P9-AGE-333

ONWARD

ENGAGING THE CULTURE
WITHOUT
LOSING THE GOSPEL

RUSSELL MOORE
BIBLE STUDY DEVELOPED BY
MICHAEL KELLEY

LifeWay Press® ★ Nashville, Tennessee

Published by LifeWay Press® ★ © 2015 Russell Moore

No part of this book may be reproduced or transmitted in any form or by any means, electronic or mechanical, including photocopying and recording, or by any information storage or retrieval system, except as may be expressly permitted in writing by the publisher. Requests for permission should be addressed in writing to LifeWay Press®; One LifeWay Plaza; Nashville, TN 37234-0152.

ISBN 978-1-4300-4033-0 ★ Item 005727825

Dewey decimal classification: 261.1
Subject headings:
CHURCH AND SOCIAL PROBLEMS \ CHRISTIANITY \ POPULAR CULTURE

Unless indicated otherwise, Scripture quotations are taken from The Holy Bible, English Standard Version® (ESV®), copyright © 2001 by Crossway, a publishing ministry of Good News Publishers. Used by permission. All rights reserved. Scripture marked NASB is taken from the New American Standard Bible®, Copyright © 1960, 1962, 1963, 1968, 1971, 1972, 1973, 1975, 1977, 1995 by The Lockman Foundation. Used by permission. *(www.lockman.org)* Scripture marked RSV is from the Revised Standard Version of the Bible, copyrighted 1946, 1952, © 1971, 1973.

To order additional copies of this resource, write to LifeWay Resources Customer Service; One LifeWay Plaza; Nashville, TN 37234-0113; fax 615.251.5933; call toll free 800.458.2772; order online at *www.lifeway.com;* email *orderentry@lifeway.com;* or visit the LifeWay Christian Store serving you.

Printed in the United States of America

Groups Ministry Publishing ★ LifeWay Resources
One LifeWay Plaza ★ Nashville, TN 37234-0152

CONTENTS

ABOUT THE AUTHOR

RUSSELL MOORE

Russell Moore is the president of the Ethics and Religious Liberty Commission of the Southern Baptist Convention, the nation's largest Protestant denomination. *The Wall Street Journal* called him "vigorous, cheerful, and fiercely articulate." Moore is the author of several books, including *Adopted for Life: The Priority of Adoption for Christian Families and Churches.* He and his wife, Maria, are the parents of five sons.

BIBLE STUDY DEVELOPED BY MICHAEL KELLEY

Michael Kelley lives in Nashville, Tennessee, with his wife, Jana, and three children: Joshua, Andi, and Christian. He serves as the director of Groups Ministry for LifeWay Christian Resources. As a communicator, Michael speaks across the country at churches, conferences, and retreats. He's the author of *Wednesdays Were Pretty Normal: A Boy, Cancer, and God; Transformational Discipleship;* and *Boring: Finding an Extraordinary God in an Ordinary Life.*

INTRODUCTION

Onward explores how the kingdom of God informs the way Christians engage the culture with the gospel. In this Bible study I talk about how engaging the culture with the claims of the resurrected Jesus Christ has never been easy. The "good old days," when people didn't question the Bible or challenge the authority of Christ, never really existed. The world is the same in that regard as it was in the garden of Eden.

But it's also true that, as Bob Dylan sang, "The times they are a-changin'." We live in a culture that's indeed undergone dramatic shifts in a remarkably short period of time. Many Christians are understandably distraught, not knowing how to carry out Christ's mission in a world they don't recognize anymore. Some Christians think we should regroup and try to be a politically weaponized moral majority once again. Some Christians think we should try to evolve on certain issues so that the culture will listen to us. Some think we should just retreat into our churches and "focus on the gospel." Who's right?

Well, Jesus is. So *Onward,* more than anything else, is about listening to what Jesus is telling us about how to live and work as citizens of His kingdom as we wait for it to come in fullness.

The project of engaging the culture while holding fast to the gospel isn't an assignment for individuals. This task wasn't given to the politicians and advocates of the world. It was given to you and me; to your local church and my local church; and to every gospel-believing, Bible-preaching local congregation throughout human history. That's why this Bible study exists: to bring Christians together across racial, ethnic, class, and all other divisions erected by sinful humanity to carry out the task our Lord began and calls us to join. None of us can go onward alone. Thankfully, none of us have to.

I hope you'll benefit from this Bible study. I hope it drives you deeper into the Scriptures and the promises of our Lord. I hope it strengthens your convictions and your conversations with the unsaved people around you. Most of all, I hope it renews your faith and confidence in the Galilean who promised that not even the gates of hell would overcome His church (see Matt. 16:18).

Onward!

HOW TO USE THIS STUDY

This Bible study provides a guided process for individuals and small groups to explore Scriptures that shape a Christian response in six key areas of cultural engagement:

KINGDOM
CULTURE
MISSION
HUMAN DIGNITY
FAMILY STABILITY
CONVICTIONAL KINDNESS

One week of Bible study is devoted to each of these topics, and each week is divided into three sections of personal study:

TEACHINGS OF JESUS
WITNESS OF SCRIPTURE
GOSPEL APPLICATION

In these sections you'll find biblical teaching and interactive questions that will help you understand and apply the teaching.

In addition to the personal study, six group sessions are provided that are designed to spark gospel conversations around brief video teachings. Each group session is divided into three sections:

START focuses participants on the topic of the session's video teaching.

WATCH provides key Scriptures presented in the video and space to take notes.

RESPOND guides the group in a discussion of the video teaching.

If you want to go deeper in your study, you may want to read the book on which this Bible study is based. *Onward* (B&H Publishing) is ISBN 978-1-4336-8617-7.

TIPS FOR LEADING A GROUP

PRAYERFULLY PREPARE

Prepare for each meeting by—
REVIEWING the weekly material and group questions ahead of time;
PRAYING for each person in the group.

Ask the Holy Spirit to work through you and the group discussion as you point to Jesus each week through God's Word.

MINIMIZE DISTRACTIONS

Create a comfortable environment. If group members are uncomfortable, they'll be distracted and therefore not engaged in the group experience. Plan ahead by taking into consideration—

> **SEATING, TEMPERATURE, LIGHTING, FOOD OR DRINK, SURROUNDING NOISE, AND GENERAL CLEANLINESS.**

At best, thoughtfulness and hospitality show guests and group members they're welcome and valued in whatever environment you choose to gather. At worst, people may never notice your effort, but they're also not distracted. Do everything in your ability to help people focus on what's most important: connecting with God, with the Bible, and with one another.

INCLUDE OTHERS

Your goal is to foster a community in which people are welcome just as they are but encouraged to grow spiritually. Always be aware of opportunities to—
INCLUDE any people who visit the group;
INVITE new people to join your group.

An inexpensive way to make first-time guests feel welcome or to invite someone to get involved is to give them their own copies of this Bible study book.

ENCOURAGE DISCUSSION

A good small-group experience has the following characteristics.

EVERYONE PARTICIPATES. Encourage everyone to ask questions, share responses, or read aloud.

NO ONE DOMINATES—NOT EVEN THE LEADER. Be sure that your time speaking as a leader takes up less than half of your time together as a group. Politely guide discussion if anyone dominates.

NOBODY IS RUSHED THROUGH QUESTIONS. Don't feel that a moment of silence is a bad thing. People often need time to think about their responses to questions they've just heard or to gain courage to share what God is stirring in their hearts.

INPUT IS AFFIRMED AND FOLLOWED UP. Make sure you point out something true or helpful in a response. Don't just move on. Build community with follow-up questions, asking how other people have experienced similar things or how a truth has shaped their understanding of God and the Scripture you're studying. People are less likely to speak up if they fear that you don't actually want to hear their answers or that you're looking for only a certain answer.

GOD AND HIS WORD ARE CENTRAL. Opinions and experiences can be helpful, but God has given us the truth. Trust Scripture to be the authority and God's Spirit to work in people's lives. You can't change anyone, but God can. Continually point people to the Word and to active steps of faith.

KEEP CONNECTING

Think of ways to connect with group members during the week. Participation during the group session is always improved when members spend time connecting with one another outside the group sessions. The more people are comfortable with and involved in one another's lives, the more they'll look forward to being together. When people move beyond being friendly to truly being friends who form a community, they come to each session eager to engage instead of merely attending.

Encourage group members with thoughts, commitments, or questions from the session by connecting through—

EMAILS, TEXTS, AND SOCIAL MEDIA.

When possible, build deeper friendships by planning or spontaneously inviting group members to join you outside your regularly scheduled group time for—

**MEALS; FUN ACTIVITIES; AND
PROJECTS AROUND YOUR HOME, CHURCH, OR COMMUNITY.**

KINGDOM
CULTURE
MISSION
HUMAN
DIGNITY
FAMILY
STABILITY
CONVICTIONAL
KINDNESS

START

Welcome the group to session 1 of *Onward*. Open your group time by asking participants to introduce themselves with a quick answer to the following questions.

What's your name, and what's one thing you're looking forward to this week?

Would you describe yourself as an optimist or a pessimist? Why?

Do you think others close to you would describe you the same way? Why or why not?

If you're a Christian, you have every reason to be an optimist. But the Christian sense of optimism isn't a hoping-for-the-best mentality; instead, it's born from the real hope afforded to us by God's promises in Christ. We can look to the future with confidence and joy because we're people who know what's coming. We're the people of God's kingdom.

Over the next six weeks we'll discover ways we as people of God's kingdom can boldly live in the present and look to the future as the kingdom marches onward.

Read together as a group Luke 4:16-21. Then watch video session 1, in which Dr. Moore starts us on the journey forward by helping us understand more about the nature of God's kingdom and who we are as kingdom citizens.

WATCH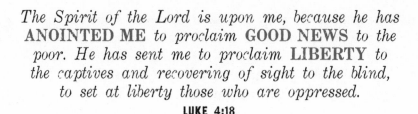

The Spirit of the Lord is upon me, because he has **ANOINTED ME** *to proclaim* **GOOD NEWS** *to the poor. He has sent me to proclaim* **LIBERTY** *to the captives and recovering of sight to the blind, to set at liberty those who are oppressed.*

LUKE 4:18

We are not contending against flesh and blood, but against the **PRINCIPALITIES**, *against the* **POWERS**, *against the world rulers of this present darkness, against the spiritual hosts of wickedness in the* **HEAVENLY PLACES**.

EPHESIANS 6:12, RSV

Seek first the **KINGDOM OF GOD** *and his* **RIGHTEOUSNESS**.

MATTHEW 6:33

FEAR NOT, *little flock, for it is your Father's* **GOOD PLEASURE** *to give you the* **KINGDOM**.

LUKE 12:32

RESPOND

For many people, the kingdom of God can be a confusing concept.

When you think about the kingdom of God, what images first come to your mind?

How did the video teaching challenge or broaden your perspective on God's kingdom?

Dr. Moore helped us see that the kingdom of God isn't only a new reality coming in the future but also a reality that's happening right now because it was inaugurated with the coming of Jesus.

Why does the fact that the kingdom is here mean we're now living in a time of war?

When have you experienced fighting and struggling as a part of God's kingdom?

How does knowing that the kingdom of God is in conflict with the kingdom of the world change the way you view your life? How does it influence the way you view the church?

If the kingdom of God is in conflict with the kingdom of the world, then conflict is natural. The church is an outpost of the true kingdom in the midst of hostile territory.

Reread Matthew 6:33. How would keeping our focus on the kingdom shape our expectations not only for our lives but also for the way we interact with the world around us?

In closing, pray and thank God for inviting us to participate in His kingdom work.

Complete the three personal-study sections on the following pages before the next group session. One section will focus on the teachings of Jesus, one on broader teachings from Scripture, and one on how to apply these teachings to our lives.

TEACHINGS OF JESUS

Have you ever wondered what made Jesus so compelling to the first people who encountered Him? There are the obvious answers, of course—His miracles, His ability to speak with unashamed, fearless authority, and His willingness to associate with people who were deemed unapproachable in that society. But there was more. As you read the accounts of Jesus' life in the Gospels, you can't escape the fact that He was advancing something so dramatic and so opposite the predominant way of thinking that it could only be described as a new kingdom.

And just as any kingdom has a certain set of cultural assumptions and expectations, so does the kingdom Jesus was ushering in. This kingdom is an upside-down kind of kingdom; it espouses a radically different way of thinking, believing, and living. Therefore, the kingdom of Jesus stands in stark contrast to the kingdoms of the earth. If we want to embrace the kingdom of God, we must begin by embracing the reality that this kingdom is unlike the kingdoms we were all born into.

Read Matthew 5:3–12. What are some differences between Jesus' kingdom and the kingdoms we were born into?

Can you think of other occasions when Jesus contradicted the popular way of thinking and believing in His time? Record some.

What do these examples show you about His kingdom?

To embrace the kingdom of Jesus, we must embrace an entirely new set of principles that guide our thoughts. Jesus was constantly urging those around Him to unlearn their patterns of thinking in favor of adopting this new set of standards. As we read His words, we hear the nearly constant refrain of "You have heard ... , but I say to you ..." This is an entry point for understanding the kingdom of God and the King who reigns there:

★ The last will be first.
★ The servant will be the leader.
★ The one who loses all will gain in the end.

You can see how the teaching of Jesus, not to mention His life, exemplified this opposite way of thinking. In a world and culture bent on accumulation, power, prestige, and self-gratification, Jesus brought a new kingdom with the opposite values. He ushered in the kingdom we were always meant to live in and love.

Of course, if Jesus was introducing a new kingdom into the existing kingdoms of the world, there would obviously be friction. Those who hungered for the prized possessions of the earthly kingdoms—power and prestige—would react violently to this intrusion. Today we must also be careful not to try and impose earthly values on this heavenly kingdom.

Read Matthew 20:20–28. In one column record characteristics of the earthly kingdom. In the other column write characteristics of the kingdom of God.

Earthly Kingdom   **Kingdom of God**

The sons of Zebedee, James and John, and their mother were having trouble reconciling their priorities with the values of this new kingdom. It's easy to understand why: they were born into a certain way of thinking, and that line of thought isn't easily swayed.

Referring to the list you made, how would you summarize the values of James, John, and their mother?

How do those values contradict the nature of the kingdom of God?

Read John 18:28–37. How are Pilate's reactions to Jesus' kingdom similar to those of James, John, and their mother?

We can see from these accounts that the introduction of a new kingdom not only challenges the status quo of the kingdoms of the earth but also threatens them. It's essential for us to recognize, as Paul later would, that we're in a time of war. However, we have to remember:

> *We do not wrestle against flesh and blood, but against the rulers, against the authorities, against the cosmic powers over this present darkness, against the spiritual forces of evil in the heavenly places.*
> **EPHESIANS 6:12**

When Jesus' kingdom clashed with the kingdoms of the world, the result was, expectedly, violent. Jesus, as the Prince and Emissary of this new kingdom, was executed by the kingdom of the world as a threat to its very existence. The same thing has been happening to those who follow His lead ever since. This shouldn't surprise us; we're living in a time of war. The declaration of the kingdom is a declaration of war.

In what sense are we, as citizens of this
new kingdom, living in a time of war?

How is this war similar to earthly
conflicts? How is it different?

We're in a war, but just as this war is different from any earthly conflict, the means
by which we wage that war are different from the weapons of earthly battles. We
can get a glimpse of these differences when we understand the nature of the
kingdom we represent.

Read the following Scripture passages. Record
how each one depicts the spiritual battle between
God's kingdom and the kingdom of darkness.

Matthew 8:16–17

Matthew 8:23–27

Mark 1:23–24

Describe the battle of the kingdom in a couple
of sentences. What do these verses teach you
about the nature of God's kingdom?

These passages, along with a host of others, don't just show us the work of Jesus; they show us the nature of the kingdom. In inaugurating the kingdom of God, Jesus was ushering in the rightful rule and reign of God. The kingdom of God reverses all the consequences that have come about because of human rebellion against His good and loving authority. In other words, embracing God's kingdom is lovingly and willingly submitting to His authority over all things.

Jesus Himself described life in the kingdom when He announced its advent in front of a waiting congregation in Nazareth. From this passage in the Book of Luke, we see that the kingdom of God is a holistic re-creation of both the spiritual and physical realms.

Read this account in Luke 4:16–21. Circle words or phrases that are signs of God's kingdom.

He came to Nazareth, where he had been brought up. And as was his custom, he went to the synagogue on the Sabbath day, and he stood up to read. And the scroll of the prophet Isaiah was given to him. He unrolled the scroll and found the place where it was written,

"The Spirit of the Lord is upon me,
because he has anointed me
to proclaim good news to the poor.
He has sent me to proclaim liberty to the captives
and recovering of sight to the blind,
to set at liberty those who are oppressed,
to proclaim the year of the Lord's favor."

And he rolled up the scroll and gave it back to the attendant and sat down. And the eyes of all in the synagogue were fixed on him. And he began to say to them, "Today this Scripture has been fulfilled in your hearing."
LUKE 4:16-21

How does this passage show that God's
kingdom is both physical and spiritual?

What's the danger if we tend to think of God's
kingdom exclusively as either physical or spiritual?

In this passage Jesus spoke of the future to which God was drawing His creation. This future had been pictured in the tabernacle and the temple, where God would draw close to His people. But it had also been pictured in the year of jubilee, a time when debts were canceled and prisoners were freed (see Lev. 25:8-55). The jubilee year of Israel signified that the existing power structures wouldn't always be as they were, that God would turn all things upside down.

The prophet Isaiah, whose words Jesus quoted, had been writing to a people weary of war and exile. He spoke of a jubilee that wouldn't be part of the cycle of a century but a new, lasting order (see Isa. 61:1-2). This would be ushered in by One whom God would anoint. The word *anointed* (see Isa. 61:1; Luke 4:18) is kingly talk. When God anointed David, for example, with the Spirit, David was empowered to take on the enemies of the people, to fight for their safety. In the reign of the coming anointed Ruler, the prisoners would find freedom; the blind would find sight; the poor would find hope; and most important of all, the favor of God would rest again on His people. This is what we're fighting for.

God's kingdom is both a spiritual and physical reality, just as it's both here and now yet still coming. Because we live in the now, however, we live in the battle of the meantime. Jesus has shown us the end to keep in mind so that we can be active in the present battle. When we take up the battle, we join with Him in bringing His kingdom even as we pray, "Your kingdom come" (Matt. 6:10).

WITNESS OF SCRIPTURE

One of the more popular messages of the earthly kingdom all of us were born into can be summarized like this: "Find yourself." This is typically an exhortation to find whatever makes you happiest, whatever brings you fulfillment, whatever you want to do and be and pursue that thing, lifestyle, person, or adventure with all the vigor you can muster.

How have you seen this message around you this week?

What are one or two areas of your life you've seen this belief try to invade?

How does this message contradict the message of God's kingdom?

Of course, there's a major fallacy in that line of thinking. The problem is that we're looking inside ourselves to find our deepest meaning and satisfaction. Implicit in that search is the idea that we actually know what would be most fulfilling and meaningful to us; it's based on the assumption that the answers to who we are and what we're doing here are actually found inside ourselves. But anyone who has the tiniest amount of self-awareness can tell you that we humans have an immense capacity to deceive ourselves. We can think we're doing one thing for the best reasons and purposes only to find out we were deceiving ourselves. We lied to ourselves, and that thing we went after with all the vigor we could muster ended up not being satisfying at all.

We promise ourselves happiness, and we deliver ourselves despair.

Can you relate to that statement? Identify a time when you were disappointed by something you heavily invested in.

Because everything about us, including our ability to know what's good and right for us, has been broken by sin, we must look outside ourselves to see who we really are and what we should really care about. It's through God's kingdom that we find out the answers to our most pressing questions. So who are we, in light of God's kingdom invasion?

Read Philippians 3:18–21 and circle words that describe those who are part of God's kingdom.

Many, of whom I have often told you and now tell you even with tears, walk as enemies of the cross of Christ. Their end is destruction, their god is their belly, and they glory in their shame, with minds set on earthly things. But our citizenship is in heaven, and from it we await a Savior, the Lord Jesus Christ, who will transform our lowly body to be like his glorious body, by the power that enables him even to subject all things to himself.
PHILIPPIANS 3:18-21

Why do you think Paul chose those words to describe us? What are some of the implications that come with terms like these?

If we begin with the knowledge that the kingdom of God is an invasion of an opposite and upside-down-minded kingdom into the existing realm of earth, we begin to clearly see why Paul used the word *citizen* to describe who we are in the kingdom.

What does it mean to be a citizen of a nation? What are some of the rights, privileges, and implications that come with that designation?

How does a person become a citizen? What does that process reveal about the kingdom of God?

Citizenship describes a person's origin and home. No matter where in the world people find themselves, they carry this identification with them. Furthermore, the most common way to become a citizen is simply a matter of birth; you're a citizen of the nation, or kingdom, into which you were born.

The same dynamics hold true in the kingdom of God. You become a citizen of God's kingdom by being spiritually born again. And just as with earthly citizenship, there are certain rights and privileges that come with spiritual citizenship in God's kingdom. This designation tells us that no matter where we are, what our vocation is, or what our present circumstances are, we have a lasting, permanent home. But the place where we currently dwell is far from it; that's why the Bible has other instructions for us as well.

Read 1 Peter 2:11–17 and circle the words Peter used to describe Christians.

Beloved, I urge you as sojourners and exiles to abstain from the passions of the flesh, which wage war against your soul. Keep your conduct among the Gentiles honorable, so that when they speak against you as evildoers, they may see your good deeds and glorify God on the day of visitation. Be subject for the Lord's sake to every human institution, whether it be to the emperor as supreme, or to governors as sent by him to punish those who do evil and to praise those who do good. For this is the will of God, that by doing good you should put to silence the ignorance of foolish people. Live as people who are free, not using your freedom as a cover-up for evil, but living as servants of God. Honor everyone. Love the brotherhood. Fear God. Honor the emperor.

1 PETER 2:11-17

How do these words inform our perspective on being kingdom citizens?

We're displaced citizens, dwelling in a land that's not our home. It's helpful in this instance to think of ourselves in terms of national diplomats who, like us, find themselves living in another land that isn't their home. Despite their nation of residency, these people live in a foreign land with a specific purpose: they're representatives of their home, emissaries of their own nation. To be true to their home country, they must represent the interests, retain the customs, and function in a way that's true to the place where they ultimately have their allegiance.

Similarly, we as Christian strangers find ourselves living in a foreign kingdom, one that's hostile in many ways to the kingdom we represent. Our customs, priorities, and values don't mesh well with our surroundings, and that's not a bad thing. It's the strangeness of Christians that sets them apart and makes them unique. If you look back at the words of Peter, you'll see that he too recognized this · unique strangeness. He didn't urge his audience to normalize their behavior, to simply fit in with the context surrounding them; instead, he urged them to maintain their distinction, knowing that the values of the kingdom they represented would be so strangely out of place that they would inevitably attract the attention of those around them.

Look back at the passage from 1 Peter. What was the goal of the lives of the Christians described there?

What are some ways we might be tempted to "normalize" our Christianity? Why is it so tempting to do so?

Look again at the text. How do you see a balance between retaining our citizenship in heaven and respecting those around us?

Peter recognized the practicality of living in a foreign land. He said, for example, that believers, as strangers and aliens in an earthly kingdom, should submit to the laws around them as much as it was possible. For Peter, it wasn't resistance to the culture that marked the followers of Christ as much as it was their good deeds and honor. In other words, they weren't marked so much by standing against the culture around them as they were by standing for the kingdom they represented.

What's the difference between being known for what you're against and being recognized for what you're in favor of?

Which do you think we tend to gravitate toward as Christians? Why?

As anyone can attest who's lived for a time in a radically different culture from the one in which they were born, it's a lonely business. At times you can feel as if you're all alone; you're the lonely voice with different interests and priorities from those around you. That's why it's helpful for us to remember that we, as God's strangers, aren't really alone.

The church is the gathering of these strangers and aliens; it's the outpost of God's kingdom. As participants not only in God's great kingdom but also in these local outposts of that kingdom, we serve a greater purpose in the cosmos than we might even be aware.

Read the following verses.

[God] put all things under [Jesus'] feet and gave him as head over all things to the church, which is his body, the fullness of him who fills all in all.
EPHESIANS 1:22-23

> *To me, though I am the very least of all the saints, this grace was given, to preach to the Gentiles the unsearchable riches of Christ, and to bring to light for everyone what is the plan of the mystery hidden for ages in God who created all things, so that through the church the manifold wisdom of God might now be made known to the rulers and authorities in the heavenly places.*
>
> **EPHESIANS 3:8-10**

How does Ephesians 1:22–23 describe Jesus and the church?

According to Ephesians 3:8–10, what's the purpose of the church?

When we gather together as the body of Christ, under Jesus as our Head, we not only become an outpost for the values and priorities of the kingdom of God in the midst of a hostile earthly kingdom, but we also become the showplace for God's wisdom to the rulers and authorities in the heavens.

It's a profound thing indeed to know that when the church comes together, we not only bear witness to the citizens of the earthly kingdoms around us, but we also bear witness to cosmic powers that we can't even see. It's as if God has put these outposts on the shelf of the universe to showcase His power and glory. In these smaller gatherings God displays His great character to any and every universal power.

Being a citizen of the kingdom of God tells us who we are and what we ought to care about. And as the strangers of God in the midst of hostile territory, we have the incredible opportunity and privilege to represent His kingdom on earth—and beyond.

GOSPEL APPLICATION

I don't know who you are, reading this page right now, but I know this. There's a cemetery plot out there somewhere, maybe not even set aside yet, waiting for your corpse. One day, no matter who you are and what you're doing, you'll be dead. And in one hundred years chances are that no one will remember your name, including the people carrying your genes in their bloodstreams. The universe seems to be conspiring against you, in everything from the natural forces that are sapping the color from your hair to the bacteria that will eventually grind your body to a maggoty pulp. The universe, it seems, isn't your friend. The universe is trying to kill you. And it will.

Indicate on the scale how often you think about the reality of death.

Never   1   2   3   4   5   Daily

How have you seen your perspective on death change as you've grown older?

What are some ways you think the knowledge of God's kingdom is changing your perspective on death?

There are different ways we might approach the reality of death. Some have a bucket-list mentality and think of all the things they want to do before they die: "I want to go skydiving," "I want to climb Mount Kilimanjaro," or "I want to see the pyramids." Of course, there's nothing wrong with doing these things, but there's something deeply wrong with the subtext behind them. What props up these bucket lists is the idea that you live only once and that because our life span is only a span of the next 10, 20, or 100 years, we'd better make the most of it.

Jesus' gospel of the kingdom reminds us that for citizens of God's kingdom, there's much, much more.

Read 1 Corinthians 15:30–32, looking closely at the end of this passage.

Why are we in danger every hour? I protest, brothers, by my pride in you, which I have in Christ Jesus our Lord, I die every day! What do I gain if, humanly speaking, I fought with beasts at Ephesus? If the dead are not raised, "Let us eat and drink, for tomorrow we die."

1 CORINTHIANS 15:30-32

What was Paul's point in relation to our perspective on trouble and difficulty in life?

In this passage Paul was in the middle of a discourse about the future resurrection of the dead for those who are in Christ. His point was that if the resurrection of the dead isn't a reality, if there's no future for us and the kingdom of God, then the best option for us would indeed be to adopt a "You live only once" philosophy. Why not? There's nothing else coming, after all, so make the most of the limited life you have.

But the gospel of the kingdom tells us there's indeed more in store for the strangers and aliens on the earth. We can't think of our present life and our future life in two segments, planning and achieving in the one and simply waiting around for the other to kick in. The gospel is more than just a ferry ticket to get us from this world to the next. The gospel is the message of holistic transformation, not only of ourselves but also of the world in which we live.

ONWARD

**What would your life look like if you saw the gospel
of the kingdom only as a ticket to heaven?**

The gospel of the kingdom ought to create in us an equal measure of urgency
in the present and anticipation of the future. That's because the gospel of the
kingdom is both a present and a future proclamation. If we start to emphasize either of those aspects to the detriment of the other, we'll find ourselves
misshapen as citizens of this kingdom.

For example, we might focus so much on the heaven that's coming that we act as
though justice and righteousness in this world are irrelevant. We have no need or
urgency to pursue the freedom of slaves, food for the hungry, or shelter for the home-
less because heaven is about worship, so why should we care what happens on earth?

Conversely, we might frantically engage with the culture around, wringing our
hands over the state of things, because we forget that the promised kingdom
is yet to come in its fullness. In either case we're expressing a worldly attitude.
When we see the word *worldly*, we might automatically think in terms of sin. But
worldliness really means being shaped and patterned by the world around us.

Read James 1:27. Underline the two commands in this verse.

*Religion that is pure and undefiled before God, the
Father, is this: to visit orphans and widows in their
affliction, and to keep oneself unstained from the world.*
JAMES 1:27

**How does this verse strike a balance between
a present focus and a future focus?**

**Do you tend to focus more on the future aspect
of the gospel or the present implications? Why?**

Jesus knew about this balance; He's the One in whom the kingdom has come. This
is why we see Jesus not only urging repentance for salvation but also alleviating the
physical suffering around Him. It's why we see Him not only preaching the gospel
of eternal salvation but also driving out the demons in the world around Him.

When we hold these truths in balance, we're recognizing the present and future
implications of the gospel both for the world around us and for ourselves. It
means we don't have the luxury of classifying certain things in our lives as
spiritual things and viewing the natural world around us as just a temporary
environment. Everything we do matters in the present and in the future.

To really understand both the present and the future aspects of the kingdom,
we have to understand the cosmic nature of the gospel of the kingdom. While
we might think of the gospel message as being about our destiny, our eternity, our
final place in either heaven or hell, Jesus' gospel goes well beyond that. The goal
of history isn't our escape to heaven but rather the merger of heaven and earth.

**Do you think most Christians would agree
with the previous statement? Why or why not?**

**What characterizes our lives if we hold the
view that we'll someday escape to heaven?**

**On the other hand, what kinds of things would
characterize our lives if we understood that the promise
of the gospel is the merger of heaven and earth?**

Read the following verses.

I saw a new heaven and a new earth, for the first heaven and the first earth had passed away, and the sea was no more. And I saw the holy city, new Jerusalem, coming down out of heaven from God, prepared as a bride adorned for her husband. And I heard a loud voice from the throne saying, "Behold, the dwelling place of God is with man. He will dwell with them, and they will be his people, and God himself will be with them as their God. He will wipe away every tear from their eyes, and death shall be no more, neither shall there be mourning, nor crying, nor pain anymore, for the former things have passed away."

REVELATION 21:1-4

What emotions do you feel when you read these verses?

What do these verses suggest about the relationship between present and future realities?

The reality of the future informs the decisions of the present. That's why every decision we make is really a gospel-informed decision. That's why decisions like the way we treat our bodies have significance; we respect the body because we believe our material bodies are part of God's goal for us and the universe. We care about the environment because we believe this world isn't ultimately going to be scrapped. We engage in issues of politics and culture because God is preparing us to rule with Christ.

At the same time, we don't make the body ultimate. We don't worship the environment. And we don't wring our hands in fretful worry at the state of the culture. A holistic view of the gospel and the kingdom frees us to pour ourselves into loving, serving, and working because these things are seeds of the tasks God has for us in eternity.

Read Romans 8:31–39. Underline all the rhetorical questions Paul asked. Then circle around the words referring to us as Christians.

What then shall we say to these things? If God is for us, who can be against us? He who did not spare his own Son but gave him up for us all, how will he not also with him graciously give us all things? Who shall bring any charge against God's elect? It is God who justifies. Who is to condemn? Christ Jesus is the one who died—more than that, who was raised—who is at the right hand of God, who indeed is interceding for us. Who shall separate us from the love of Christ? Shall tribulation, or distress, or persecution, or famine, or nakedness, or danger, or sword? As it is written,

> *"For your sake we are being killed*
> *all the day long;*
> *we are regarded as sheep to be slaughtered."*

No, in all these things we are more than conquerors through him who loved us. For I am sure that neither death nor life, nor angels nor rulers, nor things present nor things to come, nor powers, nor height nor depth, nor anything else in all creation, will be able to separate us from the love of God in Christ Jesus our Lord.

ROMANS 8:31-39

Notice the tension Paul created in this passage. Do you see it? Who can separate us from the love of Christ? Nothing in all creation, but Paul lists several things that will try. We're more than victorious, and yet we're being put to death all day long, counted as sheep to be slaughtered. This is a description of life in the kingdom in the present age.

Because of the gospel we know we're strangers and exiles in the present time. But we aren't losers. There will be "wars and rumors of wars" (Matt. 24:6)—literal and cultural—but Jesus is on the move. We fight, but we fight from triumph, not from defeat. The gospel has secured our future in the kingdom, so we now engage this conflict as members of God's victorious kingdom.

KINGDOM CULTURE

MISSION

HUMAN DIGNITY

FAMILY STABILITY

CONVICTIONAL KINDNESS

START

Welcome to session 2 of *Onward*. Open your group time by asking participants to give quick answers to the following questions.

What was one thing that stood out to you as you worked through the personal study this week?

As you think about what we've studied so far, why would you say it's important for a Christian to have a right understanding of the kingdom of God?

How do you think most Christians feel about the culture around them right now? Why?

As we saw in the previous group session, Christians are citizens of a new kind of kingdom, one with a very different culture from the world around us. The next question for us to examine, then, is how we engage the culture around us without compromising the gospel of the kingdom.

Read together as a group the prayer Jesus prayed for His first followers and for us, recorded in John 17:6-18. Then watch video session 2, in which Dr. Moore teaches about the culture both inside and outside the church.

*If my **PEOPLE** who are called by **MY NAME** humble themselves, and pray and seek my face and turn from their wicked ways, then I will hear from **HEAVEN** and will forgive their sin and heal their **LAND**.*

2 CHRONICLES 7:14

*Beloved, I urge you as **ALIENS** and **STRANGERS** to abstain from fleshly lusts which wage war against the soul.*

1 PETER 2:11, NASB

*They asked us to **REMEMBER** the **POOR**, the very thing I was eager to do.*

GALATIANS 2:10

RESPOND

Dr. Moore began his teaching by acknowledging that engaging the culture can be very confusing for Christians. Believers tend to gravitate either toward replicating the culture of the world inside the church or toward raging against the culture outside the church.

How have you seen both of these dynamics at work in the church?

Which do you tend to gravitate toward? Why?

What are the dangers of each approach?

We saw in the video teaching segment that in Luke 4 Jesus chose to focus not on the culture of the world around Nazareth but on the culture of the religious people inside the town.

Read Luke 4:16–30.

In light of the video teaching you saw, why did the people respond so violently to Jesus' proclamation?

Why is it important for us to first focus on the culture inside our churches before we engage the culture of the world outside it?

Did anything come to mind when Dr. Moore challenged us to pay attention to the issues we're currently blind to?

In closing, pray and ask God to give us wisdom and compassion in relating to our culture while remaining holy and distinctive from it.

Complete the three personal-study sections on the following pages before the next group session.

TEACHINGS OF JESUS

Let me take you back to the scene in Luke 4. Imagine it with me. Nazareth was a blip on the map of Israel; if it had a reputation at all, it was negative. There was even a proverb of the day that was something of a socioeconomic slur: "Can anything good come out of Nazareth?" (John 1:46). Well, at long last something good had.

Jesus, Mary and Joseph's son, was making a name for Himself on the preaching circuit of the day. And now that favored son of this little town was coming home.

Read Luke 4:16–17 and put yourself in the atmosphere described there.

> *He came to Nazareth, where he had been brought up. And as was his custom, he went to the synagogue on the Sabbath day, and he stood up to read. And the scroll of the prophet Isaiah was given to him. He unrolled the scroll and found the place where it was written, ...*
>
> **LUKE 4:16-17**

What do you think the vibe was like in the synagogue? How did people feel? What were they thinking?

The town was no doubt abuzz. The excitement was palpable. The people were whispering to one another, and the synagogue was packed to the brim. Standing room only. The service began with the traditional reading from the Torah, the Law, what we know today as the first five books of the Old Testament. This was a pre-scribed reading; the reader didn't choose the text he wanted but instead read from the assigned portion. As someone did the reading, people politely listened and respectfully nodded their assent to the law of their God. And that's when a hush fell over the crowd. It was time for the reading from the Law and the Prophets.

This reading was different; instead of being prescribed, it was chosen by the reader. He found his text in the scroll and then read, following the reading with his own comments and teaching. This was what they all came for. Jesus was the rabbi in town, and He started walking toward the scroll.

Let's just pause for a second here and grasp the immensity of what was happening. Jesus, the living Word, was going to read a portion of the written Word, and He was choosing that passage. So what would He choose? And then what would He say?

Continue reading this account. Underline what you think is the most significant portion of the text.

"The Spirit of the Lord is upon me,
  because he has anointed me
  to proclaim good news to the poor.
He has sent me to proclaim liberty to the captives
  and recovering of sight to the blind,
  to set at liberty those who are oppressed,
to proclaim the year of the Lord's favor."

And he rolled up the scroll and gave it back
to the attendant and sat down. And the eyes of
all in the synagogue were fixed on him. And
he began to say to them, "Today this Scripture
has been fulfilled in your hearing."
LUKE 4:18-21

How does Jesus' sermon reflect the kingdom values and priorities we studied last week?

So far, so good. If we keep reading the text, we see that the people were initially and overwhelmingly excited about the words of Jesus. But their excitement was propped up by a faulty assumption. When Jesus chose this passage from Isaiah the prophet as His text, He intentionally chose a messianic prophecy. These verses would have been very familiar to that audience; they would have known that this prophecy referred to the Promised One of God, the One who would establish God's kingdom on earth.

That's where the difficulty comes in, because the people's view of the kingdom of God was very different from that of Jesus. Their excitement turned to rage, and their endorsement turned to violence when Jesus clarified their view of the kingdom He was inaugurating.

Finish this account by reading Luke 4:22–30.

All spoke well of him and marveled at the gracious words that were coming from his mouth. And they said, "Is not this Joseph's son?" And he said to them, "Doubtless you will quote to me this proverb, 'Physician, heal yourself.' What we have heard you did at Capernaum, do here in your hometown as well." And he said, "Truly, I say to you, no prophet is acceptable in his hometown. But in truth, I tell you, there were many widows in Israel in the days of Elijah, when the heavens were shut up three years and six months, and a great famine came over all the land, and Elijah was sent to none of them but only to Zarephath, in the land of Sidon, to a woman who was a widow. And there were many lepers in Israel in the time of the prophet Elisha, and none of them was cleansed, but only Naaman the Syrian." When they heard these things, all in the synagogue were filled with wrath. And they rose up and drove him out of the town and brought him to the brow of the hill on which their town was built, so that they could throw him down the cliff. But passing through their midst, he went away.

LUKE 4:22-30

Jesus lifted up two shocking examples to illustrate the nature of the kingdom of God—a Gentile conqueror and a forgotten widow. The Nazarenes considered these people beneath them. The hometown crowd wanted a Nazarene to stand up for Nazarene values. They wanted Him to ignite a war against outsiders. But Jesus was inaugurating the kingdom God always had in mind—one that extended well beyond the dividing lines of earthly kingdoms and included the most surprising of people.

Jesus refused to bow to the cultural expectations of the people of His time; He was after a far greater kingdom than can't be confined by earthly boundaries. This desire is what drove Him to cross the cultural lines to the untouchable diseased, the forgotten downtrodden, the condemned sinners, and the hopelessly downcast. While the religious culture was content to ignore these people, confident that God would no doubt usher in the kingdom they always had in mind, Jesus obliterated their culture with His life and ministry.

> **Another powerful example of the breadth of God's kingdom is Jesus' story of the good Samaritan. Record what you can remember from Jesus' story.**

The parable of the good Samaritan (see Luke 10:25-37) is a well-worn story; it's been told and retold in countless Sunday School classes and sermons. It's been told so often, though, that we likely miss the scandalous nature of the story. The protagonist of this story was a Samaritan. In that day Israelites hated Samaritans for both historical and theological reasons. This Samaritan did what the religious leaders wouldn't, showing mercy to the victim of a crime, and Jesus lifted him up as an example.

> **When we call someone a good Samaritan today, what do we usually mean? Do you think this is what Jesus intended with this story? Why or why not?**

In telling this story, Jesus wasn't urging people to be nice and kind; He was tossing a grenade into the bunker of the religious culture of the time. The point in both Luke 4 and Luke 10 is that instead of focusing on the culture of the world, which is what the crowd in Nazareth wanted Him to do, Jesus focused on the culture inside the synagogue. Believers today must follow His lead, examining our own church culture before engaging the culture around us. Indeed, that's not only the precursor to our cultural engagement but also the means of doing so.

> **What are some questions we should ask inside the church if we want to follow Jesus in examining our religious culture?**

One of the first places we can begin examining the inside culture is by identifying ways the church has adopted the assumptions of the culture of the world. We see these assumptions in many areas of church life. Think about your church as you answer the following questions.

Whom do we primarily give leadership positions to in the church?

Are there any people groups that the church neglects? What are they?

Does the way we worship represent the uniqueness of the kingdom we're a part of? In what ways?

Are we engaging with people inside the church whom we wouldn't normally associate with apart from our link with them in the gospel? How can this engagement strengthen the church body?

These are difficult questions, and looking in the mirror can often be difficult when we're honest. If we're willing to answer them, however, we'll likely see people who, in truth, don't look much different from the kingdom of the world. Despite our sanitized version of the culture, we still elevate people to prominence based on worldly standards. We worship alongside and associate with people who look, think, get an education, and hold jobs much like us. But there are still groups of people within the church, maybe not so much like us, who are largely forgotten.

This shouldn't be so—not in the upside-down kingdom of God. The culture in the church isn't simply a sanitized version of the culture of the world. It's entirely different, with different values and different priorities. The church is where Samaritans are heroes and outsiders are welcome. The church is where the boundaries of the world are overcome by the power of the gospel.

Read the following verses and underline the boundaries the gospel crosses.

As many of you as were baptized into Christ have put on Christ. There is neither Jew nor Greek, there is neither slave nor free, there is no male and female, for you are all one in Christ Jesus. And if you are Christ's, then you are Abraham's offspring, heirs according to promise.
GALATIANS 3:27-29

Do boundary crossings like these happen without effort? Why is that important to recognize?

Paul stated an objective truth in these verses. In the kingdom of God, because of the power of the gospel, barriers that might have separated people in the kingdoms of earth have crumbled. There are no more walls of hostility. This is fact. And yet it remains for us to live out what the gospel has already done. As we focus on the culture inside the church, we'll find that many of the same boundaries, priorities, and values of the world still exist. It's left to us, then, as people of the kingdom, to actualize in the church what Jesus has achieved.

WITNESS OF SCRIPTURE

If we're willing to walk the difficult path of examining the culture inside the church, as Jesus modeled for us with the religious leaders of His day, then we'll be ready to begin discussing what engagement with the culture of the world looks like.

But as our congregations become more diverse and we start to model the kingdom more and more, we'll find that this modeling is cultural engagement in and of itself. When, for example, the church honors and cares for the vulnerable among us, we aren't showing charity. We're simply recognizing the way the kingdom really works. The child with Down syndrome on the fifth row from the back in your church isn't a ministry project. He's a future king of the universe. The immigrant woman who scrubs toilets every day on her hands and knees and can barely speak enough English to sing along with your praise choruses isn't a problem to be solved. She's a future queen of the cosmos, a joint heir with Christ.

The most important cultural witness the church has isn't, first of all, to raise up Christian filmmakers and novelists and artists and business leaders and politicians, although we ought to work to disciple and encourage believers in all sorts of callings. One of our most important cultural tasks is to crucify our worldly expectations for the church, according to which the important and the prominent inside the church walls are the same as on the outside.

Why are changes in patterns of thinking within
the church actually a form of cultural engagement?
In what ways do these changes in thinking help
us engage with the culture of the world?

Is this kind of cultural engagement
within the church harder or easier than
attacking the culture of the world? Why?

When the church embraces the "strange" nature of what it means to be citizens of the kingdom, our relationships, actions, and priorities will offer a glimpse of what life in the new kingdom will be like. We'll be speaking; we'll be engaging. Of course, the temptation is to think our cultural engagement stops there. It doesn't.

As we move out, though, we must recognize the key reality that the culture isn't something that will ever be overcome in the present age. Jesus taught us this principle in a parable.

Read the following parable of Jesus.

He put another parable before them, saying, "The kingdom of heaven may be compared to a man who sowed good seed in his field, but while his men were sleeping, his enemy came and sowed weeds among the wheat and went away. So when the plants came up and bore grain, then the weeds appeared also. And the servants of the master of the house came and said to him, 'Master, did you not sow good seed in your field? How then does it have weeds?' He said to them, 'An enemy has done this.' So the servants said to him, 'Then do you want us to go and gather them?' But he said, 'No, lest in gathering the weeds you root up the wheat along with them. Let both grow together until the harvest, and at harvest time I will tell the reapers, Gather the weeds first and bind them in bundles to be burned, but gather the wheat into my barn.' "

MATTHEW 13:24-30

List one or two questions that come to your mind when you read this parable.

What, in your own words, was Jesus trying to teach us in this story?

The story is simple enough on the surface. There were a master, a field, and an enemy. The enemy sneaked in and sowed weeds among the good seed, and the weeds began to grow. The well-meaning servants of the master had a simple solution: go out and attack the weeds. But the master had another approach in mind: the wheat and the weeds were to grow together until the time came for the harvest.

Among other things, this parable reminds us that in the field of the world, there are both wheat and weeds. We can battle against the weeds, or with patience and hope we can engage them with Christ.

This is the first understanding we must realize: all our problems with culture may not be overcome in this age. Knowing this will help us focus on the kingdom we're part of and on seeing it advance rather than raging against the old order we've come out of. We must also recognize, though, the temptation to isolate ourselves from everything around us.

Read Jesus' prayer in John 17:6–18.
Underline the specific things Jesus prayed for.

I have manifested your name to the people whom you gave me out of the world. Yours they were, and you gave them to me, and they have kept your word. Now they know that everything that you have given me is from you. For I have given them the words that you gave me, and they have received them and have come to know in truth that I came from you; and they have believed that you sent me. I am praying for them. I am not praying for the world but for those whom you have given me, for they are yours. All mine are yours, and yours are mine, and I am glorified in them. And I am no longer in the world, but they are in the world, and I am coming to you. Holy Father, keep them in your name, which you have given me, that they may be one, even as we are one. While I was with them, I kept them in your name, which you have given me. I have guarded them, and not one of them has been lost except the son of destruction, that the Scripture might be fulfilled. But now I am coming to you, and these things I speak in the world, that they may have my joy fulfilled in themselves.

I have given them your word, and the world has hated them because they are not of the world, just as I am not of the world. I do not ask that you take them out of the world, but that you keep them from the evil one. They are not of the world, just as I am not of the world. Sanctify them in the truth; your word is truth. As you sent me into the world, so I have sent them into the world.

JOHN 17:6-18

What does the fact that this prayer was prayed the night before Jesus' death tell you about the importance of these requests?

What themes do you notice emerging in this prayer?

The night before His death, our Lord had His followers on His heart, so He prayed to the Father, both for His followers of old and for those who would follow in their place (see v. 20). Among the requests He lifted up was a Christian's relationship to the world.

It's interesting to notice that Jesus not only prayed for some things but also clarified what He wasn't praying for. In verse 15 Jesus specifically prayed that God wouldn't take His followers out of the world but that He would protect us even while we're left in the midst of hostile territory. If we continue reading the prayer, we see that taking the followers of Jesus out of the world would contradict the mission Jesus was sending them on:

As you sent me into the world, so I have sent them into the world.

JOHN 17:18

In what ways do you feel the urge to separate from the world?

Think about the following areas of your life. In what ways do you most acutely feel the tension between being in the world and remaining separate from the world?

Parenting

Finances

Technology

What's the difference between being in the world and not being worldly?

It isn't Jesus' intention for the church to be an embassy protected from outside influence; it's not His will for us to build physical or metaphorical walls to protect ourselves from everything outside. Instead, He wants us to take up the commission He Himself received from the Father: to go into the world rather than isolating ourselves from the world.

Describe what it means to you that Jesus was sent into the world.

Jesus came physically. He came to extend compassion. He came to demonstrate love. And most important, He came sacrificially, giving Himself fully and completely for the sake of the world that would reject Him. This is a sobering and convicting reminder that the church doesn't exist primarily to be gathered in but to be sent out to share the witness of Christ. We're sent into the arena of modern life, all the while bearing the strangeness of the new kingdom we're citizens of. Yes, we're to hold accountable those on the inside, but we also need to engage those on the outside—with patient persuasion and mission.

What are some examples of the church's doing the exact opposite—actively holding those on the outside accountable while remaining patient with internal heresy?

The church doesn't exist merely to counter culture. The church is called to exist within the culture. We can no longer rail against political and cultural heresies on the outside but sit silently in the face of doctrinal heresies on the inside. The church must be both salt and light:

> *You are the salt of the earth, but if salt has lost its taste, how shall its saltiness be restored? It is no longer good for anything except to be thrown out and trampled under people's feet. You are the light of the world. A city set on a hill cannot be hidden. Nor do people light a lamp and put it under a basket, but on a stand, and it gives light to all in the house. In the same way, let your light shine before others, so that they may see your good works and give glory to your Father who is in heaven.*
> **MATTHEW 5:13-16**

Christians calling the church to social engagement have rightly appealed to Jesus' command for the church to be salt and light, preserving what's good and illuminating what's veiled in darkness. These images bind together the internal and external witness of the church, the call to both proclamation and demonstration.

The salt must be savory, or else it's of no use to the world (see v. 13). And the light from the church puts Christ on display for the world to see (see v. 16). Without it the presence of Christ is gone. A church that loses this distinctiveness is a church that has nothing distinctive with which to engage the culture. A worldly church is no good to the world.

GOSPEL APPLICATION

How are we sent into the world rather than remain separate from it? How do we engage the culture? Quite simply, we do it with the gospel of Jesus Christ.

The gospel isn't just the message of our salvation; neither is it simply what compels us to engage the culture in discussing all sorts of issues. The gospel also informs the tone of our engagement. We aren't prosecuting attorneys, seeking to indict our opponents with their sin. The Devil does that just fine on his own. Rather, we're defense attorneys or, as the Bible puts it, ministers of reconciliation.

Read the following verses.

From now on, therefore, we regard no one according to the flesh. Even though we once regarded Christ according to the flesh, we regard him thus no longer. Therefore, if anyone is in Christ, he is a new creation. The old has passed away; behold, the new has come. All this is from God, who through Christ reconciled us to himself and gave us the ministry of reconciliation; that is, in Christ God was reconciling the world to himself, not counting their trespasses against them, and entrusting to us the message of reconciliation. Therefore, we are ambassadors for Christ, God making his appeal through us. We implore you on behalf of Christ, be reconciled to God. For our sake he made him to be sin who knew no sin, so that in him we might become the righteousness of God.
2 CORINTHIANS 5:16-21

What, in your own words, does the term *reconciliation* mean?

Why is reconciliation the message of the gospel?

How does knowing that reconciliation is our message affect the tone of the message we deliver?

In light of the gospel, Paul first acknowledged in this passage that the entire way we view other human beings has been altered. Apart from the gospel, we might see others as opponents to be conquered or foes to be vanquished. But now, in light of the gospel of Jesus, we see everyone around us as an eternal being. Our interactions with everyone, regardless of where they're from or what station in life in which they find themselves, take on a great sense of gravity. With this new perspective we're free to treat everyone with the honor, respect, and compassion befitting another image bearer of God. But Paul didn't stop there. Because we've been reconciled to God, we now bear the message and ministry of reconciliation.

What, then, is the tone of reconciliation? It's certainly not one of hostility. Compassion, mercy, honesty, respect—these are all fitting ways to describe the tone of an ambassador of reconciliation. But Paul gives us an additional concept. He says we're imploring people to be reconciled to God (see v. 20). The word *imploring* means *pleading*.

Think about that word. What synonyms can you think of for *pleading*?

Does that term have a positive or negative connotation to you? Why?

In what sense are we pleading with those around us?

Pleading has a sense of urgency about it; in fact, the closest synonym might be *begging*. While we might initially resist the thought of begging, it helps us see just how important the task of reconciliation is. It also helps us see that we're doing something much more important and much more lasting than a piece of legislation or a form of entertainment; we traffic in matters of eternity. Remembering that encourages us to harness compassion and mercy instead of nurturing frustration and anger.

Having said that, though, we must also recognize the reality that the advance of the kingdom of God will always disrupt the kingdom of the world. Paul experienced that reality in the city of Ephesus.

Read Acts 19:21–41. Did Paul set out to change the economy of Ephesus? If not, why was the economy affected?

What does this incident teach us about the effect of kingdom advance?

Paul wasn't necessarily a political mover and shaker, and yet he found himself wound up in the politics of the day. When he arrived in Ephesus, he did what he always did in a new city: he preached the gospel. If you go back a few verses, you'll see that along with preaching, Paul performed practical signs and wonders proving the advance of the gospel of the kingdom. As more and more people believed in this message, they came to realize that certain patterns of behavior in their lives had to be dramatically altered if indeed they were to become citizens of this new kingdom.

In the city at that time, a very profitable trade grew up around idols, especially the goddess Artemis. When the people began to convert to this religion espoused by Paul, they renounced their idolatry. When they renounced their idolatry, an entire idol-making industry felt the financial pinch. What began as a spiritual awakening made its way into the practical sphere. This is what happens when we spread the gospel of the kingdom.

If we're living on mission for the sake of the kingdom, we inevitably disrupt the kingdoms of the world.

Can you relate the situation in Ephesus to any modern–day issues of idolatry?

Think about, for example, the multibillion-dollar pornographic industry at work in the world today. Of course, as Christians, we should oppose pornography, and yet we find that perhaps one of the most practical and effective ways we, as people of the kingdom, can oppose this industry is through the simple act of allowing the gospel to inform people how pornography affects the mind and the heart. When people stop looking at pornography, the pornography industry will crumble. And people will stop looking at pornography when the gospel has deeply penetrated their hearts.

The church is an alternative society, but the church is no isolated silo. Peter tells us the world is watching:

> *Beloved, I urge you as sojourners and exiles to abstain from the passions of the flesh, which wage war against your soul. Keep your conduct among the Gentiles honorable, so that when they speak against you as evildoers, they may see your good deeds and glorify God on the day of visitation.*
> **1 PETER 2:11-12**

Why do you think Peter described the church as "sojourners and exiles" (v. 11)?

List examples of how Christians can be a distraction to the gospel in the way they conduct themselves.

Why is it so important to remember our kingdom objective as we interact with those outside the church, especially when addressing issues with which we disagree?

We cultivate churches that model, always imperfectly, the kingdom of God, and from that base we speak to the outside world about the priorities of that kingdom. We don't simply advocate for the agenda of the kingdom; we embody it.

That sort of engagement necessarily creates conflict, within and without the church. Jesus kept preaching until his hometown moved from adulation to rage (see Luke 4:28-29). He then did the same thing with the rest of the nation and then on to the rest of the world. We shouldn't seek an angry, quarrelsome cultural presence, but neither should we seek to engage the culture with the sort of gospel the culture would want if they—or we—were making it up. We must understand that we can't fully reconcile Christianity and the outside culture. If the church is seeking to become relevant to those outside the church, we must do it without compromising the gospel—not on the culture's terms.

How have you seen the church become both of these extremes?

A quarrelsome cultural presence:

Seeking relevance by disregarding the gospel:

The gospel is strange. But we must continue engaging culture until the full strangeness of this message is heard. And yes, often at the root of much of our engagement with culture lies an embarrassment about the oddity of this strange biblical world of talking snakes, parting seas, and empty graves. But without that distinctive strangeness, what's Christianity for?

Jesus didn't hide the oddity of the culture of the kingdom, and neither should we. Let's listen to what our culture is saying, hearing beneath its cool veneer the fear of a people who know judgment day is coming because it's written in their hearts (see Rom. 2:15-16). Let's listen beneath the cynicism to the longings expressed in the culture, longings that can be fulfilled only in the reign of a Nazarene carpenter-king. Let's help them deconstruct the nonsense they're espousing and replace it with the truth of Scripture.

What are nonsensical things the culture sometimes presents as truth?

What are nonsensical things the church sometimes presents as truth?

What are the best ways Christians can respond to misrepresentations of the truth?

And there's more than just communicating the gospel. Let's live together in churches that call our neighbors to consider the justice and righteousness they see demonstrated among us. Let's witness—albeit imperfectly and waveringly—to what the whole universe will look like one day. Let's groan at the wreckage all around us, in this world of divorce courts and abortion clinics and gas chambers, and let's pray for the day when, as the hymn puts it:

> *Ev'ry foe is vanquished,*
> *And Christ is Lord indeed.*[1]

Let's show in the makeup and ministry and witness of our congregations what matters—and who matters—in the long run. Let's confront culture with the gospel, in all its strangeness, both inside and outside the church. And let's model what happens to a culture when the kingdom interrupts us on our way to where we'd go if we were mapping this out on our own.

Let's not merely advocate for causes; let's embody a kingdom. Let's not aspire to be a moral majority but a gospel community, one that doesn't exist for itself but for the larger mission of reaching the whole world with the whole gospel.

That sort of kingdom-first cultural engagement drives us not inward but onward.

---

1. George Duffield Jr., "Stand Up, Stand Up for Jesus," *Baptist Hymnal* (Nashville: LifeWay Worship, 2008), 657.

KINGDOM CULTURE

MISSION

HUMAN DIGNITY

FAMILY STABILITY

CONVICTIONAL KINDNESS

START

Welcome to session 3 of *Onward*. Open your group time by asking participants to give quick answers to the following questions.

What was one thing that stood out to you as you worked through the personal study this week?

As you've thought about it, how might Jesus be turning the tables on the culture inside the church right now?

In this session we'll focus on the mission of the church. In one sentence how would you describe the mission of the church?

If the church is going to engage the culture without compromising the gospel, it's imperative that we have a good understanding of our mission. The mission of the church helps us know where to expend our energy, focus our attention, and invest our resources. Without that firm sense of mission, the church will flounder in the culture rather than meaningfully engaging with it.

Read together as a group the marching orders Jesus gave His followers in Matthew 28:18-20. Then watch video session 3, in which Dr. Moore addresses the mission of the church.

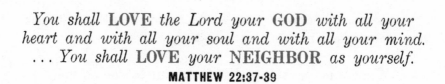

You shall **LOVE** *the Lord your* **GOD** *with all your
heart and with all your soul and with all your mind.
... You shall* **LOVE** *your* **NEIGHBOR** *as yourself.*
MATTHEW 22:37-39

The **LIGHT** *shines in the* **DARKNESS,** *and the
darkness has not overcome it. He came to his
own, and his own people did not receive him.*
JOHN 1:5,11

In **CHRIST** *God was reconciling the world to himself,
not counting their trespasses against them, and
entrusting to us the message of* **RECONCILIATION.**
2 CORINTHIANS 5:19

RESPOND

Dr. Moore emphasized that cultural engagement is often where the mission of the church gets derailed, either by being absorbed by the culture or by treating the people around us like our enemies.

Have you witnessed either of those experiences firsthand?

Why is it so easy to fall into those errors?

How can a firm understanding of and commitment to our mission guard against both of these traps?

Dr. Moore took us again to Luke 4, a passage in which Jesus' teaching first excited but then challenged the crowd. They were so challenged, in fact, that they tried to throw Jesus from a cliff.

Read Luke 4:24–30.

What's your initial reaction to the anger of the people? Why didn't Jesus destroy them instead of simply passing through them?

What does Jesus' response show you about His commitment to His mission?

What are some ways we can imitate Jesus' response when we meet hostility to the message of the gospel?

Pray, asking the Lord to focus you, your group, and your church on the mission given to you by God. Ask Him to keep you free of distractions and ask for His kingdom to come.

Complete the three personal-study sections on the following pages before the next group session.

TEACHINGS OF JESUS

A firm understanding of mission is imperative in any organization. The mission is the foundational purpose for everything an organization is about, whether it produces products, provides services, gathers people together, or advances the kingdom of God. Without a mission the organization flutters in the wind, blown this way and that by the winds of public opinion, profitability, and popularity.

The mission of an organization gives it a firm place to stand, something it can always come back to in order to answer the fundamental questions of exactly why it exists and how it's carrying out its purpose.

In a day and time when the cultural winds are blowing like a gale-force wind, the church would be wise to come back to this issue: What's our mission as the people of God in the church?

Yes, the church is to engage the world, seeking to become an agent of change for justice and righteousness. We're called to expose sin with the light of Christ (see Eph. 5:11). But this call serves the foundational mission of the church to engage the culture with the gospel of Jesus Christ.

Jesus knew that in the years following His ascension, His people would need to adopt a mission to accomplish the work of God. That's why He was very explicit when He gave His commission to the church.

Read Jesus' commission in the following verses. Underline the specific components of the mission.

Jesus came and said to them, "All authority in heaven and on earth has been given to me. Go therefore and make disciples of all nations, baptizing them in the name of the Father and of the Son and of the Holy Spirit, teaching them to observe all that I have commanded you. And behold, I am with you always, to the end of the age."
MATTHEW 28:18-20

In your own words, what mission did Jesus give in this passage?

What are some competing priorities in churches today?

Although Jesus was explicit, why do you think it's easy for the church to become sidetracked?

The first imperative for us to see in this mission is that it isn't based on the ingenuity, strength, or courage of the followers of Jesus. Instead, Jesus framed His command with the authority that had been given to Him.

Why is it important to note that this mission was given in and with the authority of Jesus (see v. 18)?

How should a recognition of Jesus' authority shape our perspective on the church's mission?

Authority seems to be in short supply in the world today. Part of the reason is that for years it seems that those who've been given authority in our world haven't treated that authority with the care and respect it deserves. Time and time again we've seen people, just like us, use the authority not for good but for personal gain and, in doing so, betray the trust of those who've willingly submitted to that authority.

The consequence is a general distrust for an office, a title, or a position that wields some measure of authority. But the authority of Jesus is different. Notice in these verses that Jesus has been given that authority. Unlike an elected official in our day, the authority of Jesus came not from a popular vote but from God Himself.

Before giving the church its marching orders, Jesus established the fact that He has the right to command. Additionally, this statement reveals exactly what Jesus is doing with His authority. He's putting His full support behind this particular mission. Consequently, any church that completely aligns itself with this mission is joining Jesus in what He's bringing about with His authority. The opposite, though, is also true. Any church that strays from this mission also strays from Jesus' backing. The mission of the church, both past as well as present and future, is to make disciples of Jesus in the entire world.

This is why when we look at our churches today, we'd be wise to consider exactly what we're doing in the world. Do we share the mission of Jesus, or somewhere along the line have we become distracted with other priorities?

What are some ways we can know the mission of a church?

How can we diagnose that mission without a spirit of pride?

Read this parallel passage about the mission of the church.

In the first book, O Theophilus, I have dealt with all that Jesus began to do and teach, until the day when he was taken up, after he had given commands through the Holy Spirit to the apostles whom he had chosen. He presented himself alive to them after his suffering by many proofs, appearing to them during forty days and speaking about the kingdom of God. And while staying with them he ordered them not to depart from Jerusalem, but to wait for the promise of the Father, which, he said, "you heard from me; for John baptized with water, but you will be baptized with the Holy Spirit not many days from now." So when they had come together, they asked him, "Lord, will you at this time restore the kingdom to Israel?" He said to them,

"It is not for you to know times or seasons that the Father has fixed by his own authority. But you will receive power when the Holy Spirit has come upon you, and you will be my witnesses in Jerusalem and in all Judea and Samaria, and to the end of the earth."

ACTS 1:1-8

What similarities and differences do you notice between this passage and the Great Commission in Matthew 28?

Not only does Jesus command the mission, but He also empowers it. The disciples, having recently experienced both debilitating failure at the crucifixion and exultant joy at the resurrection, still hadn't fully grasped the kind of King and kingdom they were serving. They asked Jesus:

Lord, will you at this time restore the kingdom to Israel?

ACTS 1:6

It makes one wonder if by this time Jesus was ready to close His eyes and start shaking His head. Mercifully, both for them and for us, Jesus stayed the course of reeducation, once again clarifying for His followers that the mission at hand wasn't one of immediate political or cultural dominance but instead one of gospel reconciliation.

Jesus redirected the disciples to the most important component of their upcoming mission—the Holy Spirit of God. Notice the link between the Holy Spirit and the mission of Jesus. The Spirit was coming, and the result would be power for the disciples to follow Jesus into the world on mission.

On the scale below, rate how often you think about the Holy Spirit.

Never   1   2   3   4   5   Constantly

When you think of the Holy Spirit, do you often think of Him in terms of the mission of Jesus? Why or why not?

We aren't just witnesses; we're empowered witnesses. We aren't just participating in the advance of a kingdom; we're doing so under the authority of a King.

But as the early church would soon find out, advancing the kingdom doesn't come without obstacles.

Read in Acts 7:54–8:4 the account of Stephen's stoning and what happened directly afterward. What did you notice about the way Stephen responded to persecution?

What does this passage show us about the extent to which we deliver the message of the gospel?

What does this passage show us about the extent to which we show the love and grace of Christ while we deliver the message of the gospel?

Before Stephen was the first Christian martyr, he was one of the first Christian deacons. He wasn't a vocational minister; instead, he was a layperson entrusted with distributing food to widows and other practical demonstrations of the gospel. When he was dragged in front of the synagogue and accused of blasphemy, he boldly preached the message of the gospel. For this he was killed.

Also notice that in Acts 8, hot on the heels of Stephen's assassination, persecution broke out against the church:

> *They were all scattered throughout the regions of Judea and Samaria. Now those who were scattered went about preaching the word.*
> **ACTS 8:1,4**

What do these verses show us about God's authority and intent for His mission to be fulfilled, even in the midst of obstacles and persecution?

God used this persecution to spread His fame beyond Jerusalem. When we fall under persecution because of clashing worldviews, we must first respond with love and mercy. Then we must acknowledge God's provision in our lives and remember Jesus' words in the Sermon on the Mount:

> *Blessed are those who are persecuted for righteousness' sake, for theirs is the kingdom of heaven.*
> **MATTHEW 5:10**

WITNESS OF SCRIPTURE

The Great Commission was the explicitly stated mission of the church, but it wasn't the introduction of that mission. The mission of Christ didn't start with the Great Commission or with the coming of the Holy Spirit at Pentecost. On those occasions the church joined a preexisting mission. Jesus sent the church because He'd already been sent (see John 20:21). With the Great Commission Jesus sent the church into the world under His authority (see Matt. 28:18). And at Pentecost Jesus bestowed power on the church to carry out this commission by pouring out on His followers the Spirit of anointing that rested on Him (see Acts 1:8).

The mission of the church was actually launched as soon as the rebellion occurred in Genesis 3.

Read these verses and underline
the question the serpent asked.

The serpent was more crafty than any other beast of the field that the LORD God had made. He said to the woman, "Did God actually say, 'You shall not eat of any tree in the garden'?" And the woman said to the serpent, "We may eat of the fruit of the trees in the garden, but God said, 'You shall not eat of the fruit of the tree that is in the midst of the garden, neither shall you touch it, lest you die.' " But the serpent said to the woman, "You will not surely die. For God knows that when you eat of it your eyes will be opened, and you will be like God, knowing good and evil." So when the woman saw that the tree was good for food, and that it was a delight to the eyes, and that the tree was to be desired to make one wise, she took of its fruit and ate, and she also gave some to her husband who was with her, and he ate. Then the eyes of both were opened, and they knew that they were naked. And they sewed fig leaves together and made themselves loincloths.

GENESIS 3:1-7

Why does the questioning of God's word lead to sin?

In what ways is this account a charge
against the character of God?

This was the hinge point of all creation. What was very good (see Gen. 1:31), existing in perfect peace and harmony in all respects, was suddenly and dramatically thrown off kilter. God's good work was flipped upside down in this single act of treason, and it all began with a temptation that had at its root a question about the character of God.

This is the true source of all sin, isn't it? On the surface we might look at any rebellion and say it was about sex. Or greed. Or power. Or even food. But dig a little deeper, and we find lurking beneath the surface of any sin a question about the character of God. The crafty serpent took what was intended for good and for the protection of God's beloved children and perverted it into a challenge to His love and generosity.

Can you hear the voice behind the serpent's seemingly innocent question? That voice was leveling charges against the King: "This King is stingy. He's holding back the best from you. If He really loved you, He wouldn't have issued such a limiting prohibition." Sin is more than making a bad choice; it's rooted in the character assassination of the King.

Have you ever thought about sin that way before?

How does doing so heighten the nature of rebellion?

Think about your life. Are you believing any lies about
the character of the King that are leading to sin?

The way to beat back temptations like these is with the truth of who we know God to be. Adam and Eve, however, gave in to temptation and chose to sell their birthright, as all human beings have done ever since.

Read Genesis 3:8–24. How did the man and the woman try to deal with their sin? Why was that insufficient?

List all the actions the man and the woman took in one column. In the other column list the spiritual and/or emotional motivations behind each action.

Actions   Motivations

The man and woman tried to cover up their nakedness from their newly felt shame. Then they tried to hide because of their newly realized fear. The freedom and peace that once characterized their existence were gone, and they were beginning to realize the consequences of their rebellion. Those consequences weren't limited to them alone.

List the other effects of sin given in Genesis 3:8–24.

What do these results tell you about the level of corruption in the world since the fall?

This was cosmic rebellion; it was eternal treason. And all creation was affected. Our environment, our relationships with one another, our work, and especially our connection to the King were all corrupted in the fall. Until we understand the full nature and drastic predicament in which we find ourselves, we'll be tempted to think of the gospel as a fix to our problem. To do this is to sell the nature of the gospel far, far short.

Because this was indeed a cosmic rebellion, we needed a cosmic solution. Because every arena of life as we know it was affected, the only solution would have to encompass every area of life. Because the scope of the curse was holistic in its destruction—personal, cosmic, social, and vocational—the gospel must also be holistic in its reconciliation—personal, cosmic, social, and vocational.

Think about those categories. Beside each one record an example of how you've seen the effects of sin in that area.

Personal

Cosmic

Social

Vocational

Anytime we look inside ourselves, at the world around us, or at the systems inside that world and think, *This isn't how it should be,* we're observing the effects of sin. But from the very outset God was committed to bringing all things back to their proper and right order. We see this plan begin to unfold even in the garden.

In Genesis 3 what did God do that showed His commitment to set everything as it should be?

How did God's covering of Adam and Eve foreshadow what He'd eventually do in Christ?

God called His hiding children out into the open. Observing their feeble attempts at self-covering, He Himself alleviated their shame by creating clothes for them.

These clothes came at a cost; blood had to be shed for the humans to be covered. In the New Testament Paul reminds us:

As many of you as were baptized into Christ have put on Christ.
GALATIANS 3:27

As in the first garden, we've been clothed with a sacrifice. A death occurred so that our shame could be removed. But our clothing is much better than the skin of animals; our clothing is the righteousness of Christ.

If we fast-forward to the end of the story, from Genesis to Revelation, we see that God not only reverses the effects of sin in us personally but is also on a mission to reverse the curse in a holistic manner:

I saw a new heaven and a new earth, for the first heaven and the first earth had passed away, and the sea was no more. And I saw the holy city, new Jerusalem, coming down out of heaven from God, prepared as a bride adorned for her husband.
REVELATION 21:1-2

Notice in this passage about the end of this age that we aren't escaping earth to go to heaven; instead, heaven is coming down to earth, redeeming and reshaping everything here. This mission, ultimately fulfilled in these verses, has a personal, cosmic, social, and vocational effect.

Continue reading in Revelation 21.

I heard a loud voice from the throne saying, "Behold, the dwelling place of God is with man. He will dwell with them, and they will be his people, and God himself will be with them as their God. He will wipe away every tear from their eyes, and death shall be no more, neither shall there be mourning, nor crying, nor pain anymore, for the former things have passed away." And he who was seated on the throne said, "Behold, I am making all things new." Also he said, "Write this down, for these words are trustworthy and true." And he said to me, "It is done! I am the Alpha and the Omega,

*the beginning and the end. To the thirsty I will give from
the spring of the water of life without payment. The one who
conquers will have this heritage, and I will be his God and
he will be my son. But as for the cowardly, the faithless, the
detestable, as for murderers, the sexually immoral, sorcerers,
idolaters, and all liars, their portion will be in the lake that
burns with fire and sulfur, which is the second death."*

REVELATION 21:3-8

Which part of this future state is the most meaningful to you? Why?

We might be rightly excited about many components of the fulfillment of this mission, but we should recognize that all the greatness and perfection of the future is contingent on God's dwelling with His people (see v. 3). The reason there will be no more sadness or crying, grief or pain, is because of the unbridled, unshadowed, unfiltered presence of God.

John's vision continues in the next chapter of Revelation. Here, unlike in Genesis 3, the picture is of a city:

*The angel showed me the river of the water of life,
bright as crystal, flowing from the throne of God and
of the Lamb through the middle of the street of the city;
also, on either side of the river, the tree of life with its
twelve kinds of fruit, yielding its fruit each month. The
leaves of the tree were for the healing of the nations. No
longer will there be anything accursed, but the throne of
God and of the Lamb will be in it, and his servants will
worship him. They will see his face, and his name will
be on their foreheads. And night will be no more. They
will need no light of lamp or sun, for the Lord God
will be their light, and they will reign forever and ever.*

REVELATION 22:1-5

We're on the mission to the city, and when we get there, the light at long last will have driven out all the darkness.

GOSPEL APPLICATION

We've seen that sin is far deeper and more widespread than making a few bad choices and getting off track. Instead, sin is a universal condition affecting every arena of our personal, public, and environmental existence. Although the extent of sin and its devastating effects might push us to despair, we find glorious hope in the gospel.

If the bad news of sin is worse than we imagined, the good news of the gospel is far better than we dared to hope. The gospel isn't just for us at a personal level; the gospel also reconciles all things to God. Paul commented on this reality in a number of passages, but this is one of the most vivid:

The creation waits with eager longing for the revealing of the sons of God. For the creation was subjected to futility, not willingly, but because of him who subjected it, in hope that the creation itself will be set free from its bondage to corruption and obtain the freedom of the glory of the children of God. For we know that the whole creation has been groaning together in the pains of childbirth until now. And not only the creation, but we ourselves, who have the firstfruits of the Spirit, groan inwardly as we wait eagerly for adoption as sons, the redemption of our bodies.
ROMANS 8:19-23

Underline the two sources of groaning mentioned in these verses.

What do you think it looks like for creation to groan?

What about you personally? What does it look like for you to groan within yourself?

Tornadoes, earthquakes, drought—these are groanings. They're the environmental equivalent of the response we have when we, like Paul, become frustrated at our seeming inability to act in righteousness. We all groan for something more, something better, something right, and this is what the gospel promises us.

The healing brought by the gospel is holistic. We go wrong, then, when we begin to segment the gospel instead of embracing its holistic message for the world. One way we might do this is a personal one. There was a time in evangelical churches when the gospel was seen as walking an aisle, praying a prayer, and signing a membership card. When you complete these easy steps, eternity is secure. The result is that many people are living in a terrible state of self-deception. We've believed the lie that the gospel is about the future with no effect on or implications for the present. Or we've believed the gospel is a magic formula that we can chant over and over again without considering the life-altering impact that truly believing such a message has for us.

Read the end of Peter's sermon in Acts 2 and underline the appropriate response to the preaching of the gospel that Peter prescribed.

When they heard this they were cut to the heart, and said to Peter and the rest of the apostles, "Brothers, what shall we do?" And Peter said to them, "Repent and be baptized every one of you in the name of Jesus Christ for the forgiveness of your sins, and you will receive the gift of the Holy Spirit. For the promise is for you and for your children and for all who are far off, everyone whom the Lord our God calls to himself." And with many other words he bore witness and continued to exhort them, saying, "Save yourselves from this crooked generation."
ACTS 2:37-40

What, in your own words, does it mean to repent?

Do you think repentance is a popular message today? Why or why not?

Typically, we think of repentance as stopping an action or an attitude. But *repent* doesn't mean *to stop;* the word *repent* means *to turn.* The word picture calls to mind someone who's walking in one direction, then turns the opposite way and goes that way instead. When Peter told this crowd that had come under conviction that they needed to repent, he was issuing a directive to turn away from their old way of life, their old way of thinking, and their old way of believing. The opposite direction to which they were to turn was to walk in obedience to Christ, and the the first step of obedience after repenting of their sin was to be baptized, publicly identifying themselves as followers of Jesus.

When we believe the gospel, there's a holistic kind of repentance that must characterize our lives, as well as a corresponding turning to a completely new way of life. On a personal level we might undermine this command and process in one of two ways.

1. We might fail to fully turn *from* something. In this case we might try to cling to our old patterns of thinking and behavior.

2. We might fail to fully turn *to* something. In this case we might neglect the holistic impact the gospel has on our new life in Christ.

We battle both of these fallacies the same way: by understanding the full impact, as much as we're able, of what's happened to us when we believed the gospel.

Read 2 Corinthians 5:17 and underline the way Paul describes a Christian.

If anyone is in Christ, he is a new creation. The old has passed away; behold, the new has come.
2 CORINTHIANS 5:17

How does remembering you're a new creation help you battle the tendency to cling to what you've turned from?

How does it help you fully embrace what you've turned to?

This verse describes something much different from merely praying a prayer or walking an aisle; Paul says we're a new creation in Christ. The old is gone, and the new has come. When we believe the gospel, the old person we were is uprooted, and a new person remains. That's why Jesus, when the Pharisee Nicodemus asked Him about inheriting the kingdom of God, compared it to being "born again" (John 3:3).

We're born again, not of human flesh but of the Spirit. When we are, everything about us is new. We have a new name. A new family. New tastes. New desires. The old is gone, and the new has come. The implications of this reality are staggering.

It means anytime we revert to the worldly patterns of our first birth, it's as if we're denying our true, new selves in Christ; we put on a mask when we sin. Like actors, we assume an identity that isn't true to ourselves. This is why throughout his letters Paul reminded the churches of the New Testament that they'd been made new people in Christ. Therefore, their behavior should be consistent with their identity.

Read Paul's words to the Colossians and underline ways Paul reminded them of who they were in Christ.

If then you have been raised with Christ, seek the things that are above, where Christ is, seated at the right hand of God. Set your minds on things that are above, not on things that are on earth. For you have died, and your life is hidden with Christ in God. When Christ who is your life appears, then you also will appear with him in glory. Put to death therefore what is earthly in you: sexual immorality, impurity, passion, evil desire, and covetousness, which is idolatry. On account of these the wrath of God is coming. In these you too once walked, when you were living in them. But now you must put them all away: anger, wrath, malice, slander, and obscene talk from your mouth. Do not lie to one another, seeing that you have put off the old self with its practices and have put on the new self, which is being renewed in knowledge after the image of its creator.
COLOSSIANS 3:1-10

ONWARD

In what ways should the reality of the Colossians' new life in Christ have affected their behavior?

It's a little curious when you first look at it. In verse 3 Paul said, "You have died." That's a past-tense reality, something that's come and gone. But then in verse 5 he said they must "put to death" certain things in their lives. The link between the internal reality and the external effect is the word *therefore*. You died; therefore, put to death. Let every area of your life reflect the change that's occurred in you through Christ.

Another way to think of holistic change through the gospel is in terms of indicatives (what God has already done) and imperatives (what we're supposed to do). The gospel indicative is that we have died to our old selves and have been born anew in Christ. The gospel imperatives are the commands Paul lists: putting to death "sexual immorality, impurity, passion, evil desire, and covetousness" (v. 5). The indicative drives the imperatives, and those imperatives extend to all areas of our lives.

Our mission in the world includes the mission inside ourselves. We'll be ineffective ambassadors and impotent emissaries if we fail first to apply the gospel imperatives to our whole selves. This isn't a one-time action but rather a continual recognition of habits, traits, and thought patterns we tend to turn back to even as new creations in Jesus.

For every area of our lives, we must ask over and over again, "What does the gospel say?" When we do that, we'll find that the gospel is more than a message about heaven and hell; it's a message for our entire selves.

Try this exercise for yourself. In each area of your life listed below, record one gospel imperative that applies.

Marriage

Parenting

Finances

Commitment to church

Work

The list could go on and on, and indeed it does. The gospel isn't just taking ground in the world around us; it's discovering and exploring the territory inside us that Jesus has already laid claim to and taken hold of. When we're willing to embrace the holistic nature of the gospel, both in the world and in ourselves, we'll find ourselves living what we've already become in Christ.

If we return to 2 Corinthians, we find another set of imperatives and indicatives.

Read 2 Corinthians 5:18–21 and underline each reference to the mission we've been given. Then go back and circle what God has already done.

All this is from God, who through Christ reconciled us to himself and gave us the ministry of reconciliation; that is, in Christ God was reconciling the world to himself, not counting their trespasses against them, and entrusting to us the message of reconciliation. Therefore, we are ambassadors for Christ, God making his appeal through us. We implore you on behalf of Christ, be reconciled to God. For our sake he made him to be sin who knew no sin, so that in him we might become the righteousness of God.

2 CORINTHIANS 5:18-21

We're reminded here that the imperative (what we're supposed to do) doesn't come without the indicative (what God has already done). Without being reminded that "Christ reconciled us to himself" (v. 18), we'd start to think the mission is about us and fail to become the ministers of reconciliation and the ambassadors for Christ that Paul calls us to be. Remember that God is "making his appeal through us" (v. 20). Our mission is to give ourselves completely to the mission of making Jesus known everywhere to everyone—even if it costs us everything.

This message is paramount. This message is urgent:

Behold, now is the favorable time; behold, now is the day of salvation.

2 CORINTHIANS 6:2

KINGDOM CULTURE MISSION

HUMAN DIGNITY

FAMILY STABILITY

CONVICTIONAL KINDNESS

START

Welcome to session 4 of *Onward*. Open your group time by asking participants to give quick answers to the following questions.

What was one thing that stood out to you as you worked through the personal study this week?

What are some ways we can make sure our church is focused on God's mission without being sidetracked?

In this session we'll discuss the issue of human dignity. What are some challenges to human dignity you see in the world around you?

So far we've discussed God's kingdom, the culture inside and outside our churches, and the mission God has given us to engage the culture without compromising the gospel. As we continue to focus on the mission of the kingdom, we encounter specific issues in which we can bear witness for the gospel. One of these is the issue of human dignity.

Read together as a group Genesis 1:26-31. Then watch video session 4, in which Dr. Moore teaches on human dignity.

God created man in his own image,
in the **IMAGE OF GOD** *he created him.*
GENESIS 1:27

Truly, I say to you, as you did it to one of the
LEAST OF THESE *my brothers, you did it to me.*
MATTHEW 25:40

Consider your calling, brothers: not many of you
were **WISE** *according to worldly standards, not many*
were powerful, not many were of **NOBLE** *birth.*
1 CORINTHIANS 1:26

RESPOND

As we saw in the video, truly understanding and committing to human dignity is rooted in understanding what it means to be created in God's image.

Why is this the case?

What are some areas of life in which you can see human dignity and the sanctity of human life being challenged today?

Why does a disregard for life, as Dr. Moore stated, ultimately come from pride?

Dr. Moore also helped us see that issues of human dignity go beyond the specific issue of abortion, extending to all people in our world who are forgotten and overlooked.

Why must we place value on people not based on their utility but instead on the image of God in which they were created?

Were there any segments of society you heard mentioned that don't typically come to mind when you think about this issue?

Why does God identify so closely with groups of people who are ignored and mistreated in our world?

Pray, thanking God that He identifies with the least of these in our world. Ask Him for the mercy and compassion to have that same identification with people who need our compassion and care. Pray that this week our eyes will be opened to groups in our world who are being overlooked or abused.

Complete the three personal-study sections on the following pages before the next group session.

TEACHINGS OF JESUS

There was a point in human history, during the days of the Roman Empire, when the church was regarded as the institution of women and slaves, two largely ignored and disdained groups of people during the first century. They weren't treated as whole persons but rather as pieces of property and currency. These were precisely the people welcomed into the life of the early church.

Attitudes that were meant as an insult were actually a badge of honor for the church. Disenfranchised people were not only welcomed and treated with kindness in the church; they were actually regarded with importance and prominence. This radical way of viewing people reflected the values of the kingdom of God, the kingdom that stands contrary to the patterns of the world. As these early church members lived the values of the kingdom, they followed the example of their Lord, who had inaugurated and perfectly embodied the values of that kingdom.

Read the following account illustrating Jesus' approach to someone in need.

When Jesus returned, the crowd welcomed him, for they were all waiting for him. And there came a man named Jairus, who was a ruler of the synagogue. And falling at Jesus' feet, he implored him to come to his house, for he had an only daughter, about twelve years of age, and she was dying. As Jesus went, the people pressed around him. And there was a woman who had had a discharge of blood for twelve years, and though she had spent all her living on physicians, she could not be healed by anyone. She came up behind him and touched the fringe of his garment, and immediately her discharge of blood ceased. And Jesus said, "Who was it that touched me?" When all denied it, Peter said, "Master, the crowds surround you and are pressing in on you!" But Jesus said, "Someone touched me, for I perceive that power has gone out from me." And when the woman saw that she was not hidden, she came trembling, and falling down before him declared in the presence of all the people why she had touched him, and how she had been immediately healed. And he said to her, "Daughter, your faith has made you well; go in peace."

LUKE 8:40-48

Look at Jesus' question midway through this passage. Do you think Jesus didn't know who touched Him? If He did know, why would He ask that question?

Record Peter's response to Jesus in your own words.

Jesus, while on his way to a prominent synagogue leader's house, had an encounter that illustrates His commitment to human dignity. The crowds were pressing in; in fact, the people were so thick around Him and His disciples that they were almost crushing Him. That gives us some understanding of Peter's response to Jesus' question.

When Jesus asked, "Who was it that touched me?" (v. 45), Peter more or less rolled His eyes and said something like "The real question is who *didn't* touch You. In case You haven't noticed, we're being crammed together on all sides." Of course, the context provides the answer to Jesus' question. A woman, sick with an issue of blood and destitute from spending all she had trying to be cured, was the culprit.

This woman, however, was suffering from much more than a physical malady; she was suffering from the communal humiliation that came with it. A disease like this would have caused her to be ostracized from the rest of the Jewish community; she would have been regarded as untouchable. Already a woman, a second-place citizen to begin with, she was now a pariah. She existed in the shadows—forgotten, overlooked, and even hated. It's no wonder she crept up from behind to touch only Jesus' robe; someone like this wouldn't dare approach from the front. Her intent was to quietly, discreetly, without anyone noticing, just feel the hem of Jesus' clothing. What could it hurt? She had nothing to lose. But Jesus wasn't content to let her stay in the shadows; He would not only heal her but also bring her from the darkness into the light.

Knowing these things, would you change your answer about why Jesus asked who touched Him? What was His intent with this question?

How does this story illustrate Jesus' commitment to people who are forgotten by society?

When the woman was found out, she came trembling forward. It's no wonder she was trembling; these were the same people who'd treated her as subhuman for the past 12 years, and now she was being called to stand in front of them. Yet this is precisely what Jesus had in mind. When she came out of hiding, Jesus then uttered one word that lifted up her soul and arrested the crowd's attention: "Daughter" (v. 48).

Why was Jesus' use of this term significant?

How would this word have made the woman feel?

How do you think everyone else in the crowd responded?

People like this woman—those who live in the shadows, thrown away and deemed worthless and seemingly useless—are the sons and daughters of the King. As Peter noted, she certainly wasn't the only one touching Jesus; surely she wasn't the only one who needed something from Him. But she was the only one who made Him stop.

We could continue through the life of Jesus and find many other examples just like her—tax collectors, children, the poor, sinners—these were the people who arrested the attention of Jesus as the crowd continued to press in on Him. In the eyes of Jesus, human dignity isn't determined by social standing, educational level, or any other mark of prominence conferred by the kingdoms of the earth. Instead, Jesus recognized that human dignity isn't based on someone's usefulness but on God's image.

List groups of people our world has disregarded because of their level of utility.

What about you? Is there a particular group of people you tend to think negatively about? What does this reveal about the way you see yourself and the way you see the kingdom of God?

As the end of Jesus' life drew near, as if to underscore the importance of the lowest and least, Jesus told a story that unequivocally showed us the importance of the neglected and disregarded in God's eyes.

Read Matthew 25:31–46. What was Jesus' main point in this story?

What does Jesus' choice of these actions of the sheep and the goats reveal about the value of humans?

This passage shows us just how close these people are to the heart of God. The question we might ask next, then, is why. Why do these groups of people matter so much?

This answer is foundational to our understanding of human dignity. These people matter because they're created in God's image. Their worth and value don't come from what they can contribute to society but from the fact that God has uniquely created and crafted them. Because every human being is made in His image, every human being has worth and value and is worthy of respect and dignity.

This worth extends beyond age, race, or mental capacity. The way we as Christians and as churches respond to people who've been regarded as untouchable by the rest of the world is a clear measure of whether we truly understand the kingdom of God.

Read 1 Corinthians 1:18–25.

The word of the cross is folly to those who are perishing, but to us who are being saved it is the power of God. For it is written,

I will destroy the wisdom of the wise, and the discernment of the discerning I will thwart.

Where is the one who is wise? Where is the scribe? Where is the debater of this age? Has not God made foolish the wisdom of the world? For since, in the wisdom of God, the world did not know God through wisdom, it pleased God through the folly of what we preach to save those who believe. For Jews demand signs and Greeks seek wisdom, but we preach Christ crucified, a stumbling block to Jews and folly to

Gentiles, but to those who are called, both Jews and Greeks, Christ the power of God and the wisdom of God. For the foolishness of God is wiser than men, and the weakness of God is stronger than men.

1 CORINTHIANS 1:18-25

How are the principles of Jesus' story replicated in these verses?

Why is God committed to turning the tables on the wisdom and power of this age?

Through God's commitment to the disregarded and outcast in the eyes of the world, we see once again that His kingdom stands contrary to the values and priorities of the world. What the world regards as weak, foolish, and untouchable—this is the wisdom of God in the kingdom. Of course, the ultimate example of the kingdom's upside-down values is the cross of Jesus—"Christ crucified" (v. 23).

The cross—the instrument of shame, the tool of torture, the inflictor of death—is the glory, inheritance, and life of those who follow Jesus.

WITNESS OF SCRIPTURE

No one has a firmer grasp of the issue of human dignity than Jesus Christ. With both His life and His teaching He showed us what it means to value humanity the way God values humanity. Of course, His commitment to human value culminated in the willing sacrifice of Himself on the cross.

As Paul would later comment:

> *While we were still weak, at the right time Christ died for the ungodly. For one will scarcely die for a righteous person—though perhaps for a good person one would dare even to die—but God shows his love for us in that while we were still sinners, Christ died for us.*
> **ROMANS 5:6-8**

In the previous passage highlight the terms Paul used to refer to us.

How does this language highlight Jesus' actions?

Paul pulled no punches when commenting on humanity in these verses. We were helpless; we were ungodly; we were sinners. This accurate and blistering depiction of humanity serves to bring out the great love and compassion of God in Christ.

Underscoring all the compassion, mercy, and self-sacrificial love Jesus showed in His life and death is the fact of human dignity. Jesus had a clear picture of what, ironically, often eludes us in our age of rights and privileges for human beings: that every single person was created in the image of God, and therefore every human being has great worth and value. If we want to follow Jesus in His regard for human worth, then, we must also follow Him in His understanding of what it means to be created in God's image.

What do you think it means to
be created in the image of God?

What are some of the implications of that fact?

What are some reasons we might lose sight
of that fact as we look at other people?

Let's journey back to the very beginning, to the first days of creation as God called order out of chaos and beauty out of nothingness. He began His creative work with the light illuminating the darkness and then progressed through all the things that are now visible in that light. He separated the waters from the land and brought forth vegetation and all kinds of swimming, creeping, and crawling animals. As you read Genesis 1, the familiar refrain comes again and again after each act of creation: "It was good."

Read the following passage and underline what's different about God's pronouncement after this act of creation.

God said, "Let us make man in our image, after our likeness. And let them have dominion over the fish of the sea and over the birds of the heavens and over the livestock and over all the earth and over every creeping thing that creeps on the earth."

So God created man in his own image, in the image of God he created him; male and female he created them.

And God blessed them. And God said to them, "Be fruitful and multiply and fill the earth and subdue it, and have dominion over the fish of the sea and over the birds of the heavens and over every living thing that moves on the earth." And God said, "Behold, I have given you every plant yielding seed that is on the face of all the earth, and every tree with seed in its fruit. You shall have them for food. And to every beast of the earth and to every bird of the heavens and to everything that creeps on the earth, everything that has the breath of life, I have given every green plant for food." And it was so. And God saw everything that he had made, and behold, it was very good. And there was evening and there was morning, the sixth day.

GENESIS 1:26-31

Why is God's pronouncement significant? What does this tell you about the nature of human beings?

How does that pronouncement build a framework for human dignity?

Plants? Good. Trees? Good. Animals? Good. But when we come to the issue of human beings, God said it was very good (see v. 31). What was good before was now very good. Humanity is the crown jewel in God's creation because human beings alone possess the unique characteristic of being made in God's image.

So what exactly does that mean? Scholars have debated for generations. We can say with certainty, though, that humanity is distinct from the rest of nature, including the rest of the living creatures, because we bear the image of God.

At least in part, bearing the image of God means humans have a unique relational capacity both with God and therefore with one another. We see this characteristic in later verses when man and woman walked in the garden in a state of unbroken fellowship with God. It's for this purpose we were created: to know God and enjoy Him forever. The image of God isn't something we acquire through education, status in life, or prominence in society; rather, it's an attribute God gives to all human beings. It's about who we are, not just about what we do.

That means every human being we encounter, from the lowest and the least to the most important in society, has the potential to relate to God in an intimate way. Furthermore, it also means as image bearers, humans are uniquely equipped to carry out the mission God assigned us in Genesis 1.

Look back at Genesis 1:26–31 and summarize God's instructions to humanity in these verses.

What does God's assignment indicate about human worth and dignity?

When God created humanity, He created rulers. Their role in the world was to subdue the earth, fill it, and rule over it. But they weren't to rule just for the sake of ruling; their rule wouldn't be characterized by power grabs and selfish ambition. Instead, as His image bearers, man and woman would rule justly, compassionately, and lovingly. In other words, they would reflect His image in the world God created. They would be His emissaries on earth, ruling as He sovereignly rules over the universe.

What an incredible privilege. What an amazing responsibility. And this original intent reminds us of what God is doing to this day. Christians, though currently strangers and aliens in the world, are destined to rule once again alongside Christ. The image bearers will sit alongside Jesus, the exact representation of God, as rulers of the universe.

Of course, the Enemy hates humankind for the same reason we must value and respect humankind: because of this unique trait of being made in God's image. The Devil hates us because he knows who we are. As the story continued after the fall in Genesis 3, we see that the exploitation and murder of innocent human life was one of the first wicked manifestations of that fall.

Read the account of Cain and Abel in
Genesis 4:8–16 and answer the following questions.

What caused this murder to happen?

What shift in the value of human life
do you see in these verses?

What does God's response tell you
about His opinion of human life?

The first murder is only one generation after the fall. So quickly did the value of humanity degenerate that we see this fratricide only one chapter later in Scripture, and it didn't stop there. Later in Genesis 4 we see Lamech dole out vigilante-style justice and then celebrate doing so with a song (see vv. 23-24). Pause for a second to realize the significance of this: Adam and Even were still alive, still remembering the days of the garden, and then bore witness not only to murder but also to the celebration of it.

The list goes on. The covenant of God with creation after the flood in Noah's time includes a warning against bloodshed, set in the context of human dignity as a reflection of God's image:

Whoever sheds the blood of man,
by man shall his blood be shed,
for God made man in his own image.
And you, be fruitful and multiply, increase
greatly on the earth and multiply in it.
GENESIS 9:6-7

As the children of Abraham moved toward the initial down payment on our inheritance, God forbade them from pursuing Canaanite idolatry, specifically denouncing by name the god Moloch, who demanded the violent sacrifices of human babies (see Lev. 20:1-8). The Israelites themselves were threatened with death as Pharaoh sought to strangle the people of promise in the cradle with mass murder (see Ex. 1:15-16). That same spirit was at work at the dawn of the new covenant when another king, threatened by the prophesied rule of a baby from the house of David, sought to destroy innocent infant life (see Matt. 2:16-18).

What are some of the Devil's lies that humans must believe in order to place little value on human life?

When people devalue human life, what must they believe about God? About themselves?

What lies do you see in our society that try to justify disrespect for human life?

At every point in biblical history, God mandated not only the saving of life from murder but also the protection of people who are vulnerable—the poor, the sojourner, the widow, the fatherless, and the diseased. If we're to join Him in this effort, we must also confront the lies we've believed about human worth and dignity. We must stand against the lie that value is determined by utility. We must stand against the lie that we, who exist outside the womb or might have a firm 401(k) in place, are independent and self-sustaining. In the end we must stand against the lie that we're better than everyone else.

No wonder Paul said when our minds are renewed by the gospel:

We regard no one according to the flesh.
2 CORINTHIANS 5:16

No matter whom we encounter, whether they're rich or poor, minimum wage or tenured, educated or uneducated, they've all been created in God's image. If they're in Christ, they're destined to sit with Him, ruling over creation.

GOSPEL APPLICATION

When we talk about issues of human dignity, the most obvious touch point for society today is the issue of abortion. The evil that is abortion rightly receives an incredible amount of attention and dialogue. From start to finish, the Word of God affirms the sanctity of human life and condemns the devaluing of life created in God's image.

We'd do well, however, to make sure our position is grounded in a holistic view of human dignity, of which the issue of abortion is an important component. The gospel demands that we have a holistic approach to human dignity, whether that dignity is being robbed from the unborn, the elderly, or another denigrated group of people in society. When we see an issue through that wide-angle lens, we'll find that the church has confronted this issue in various forms since its inception in the Book of Acts. That's because inside all of us is the great sense of pride that tends to measure human value by a person's utility.

Valuing people by their utility exposes the great sin of comparison. When someone is less useful, talented, or capable in the measure of the world than we are, we assign them less value. This tendency is an affront to the gospel, which reminds us that Jesus died for precisely those who are overlooked and neglected in our culture.

Why is comparing ourselves with other people contrary to the gospel?

Why are we so strongly tempted to compare ourselves with others?

Read the following verses from 1 Corinthians 5.

Don't you know that the unrighteous will not inherit God's kingdom? Do not be deceived: No sexually immoral people, idolaters, adulterers, or anyone practicing homosexuality, no thieves, greedy people, drunkards, verbally abusive people, or swindlers will inherit God's kingdom. And some of you used to be like this. But you were washed, you were sanctified, you were justified in the name of the Lord Jesus Christ and by the Spirit of our God.

1 CORINTHIANS 5:9-11

Why did Paul remind the Corinthians that they too once committed the same sins he listed?

The church at Corinth needed to remember this. The first part of this chapter described the church as being very litigious; lawsuits were being thrown this way and that, and Paul wanted these believers in Christ to settle matters without involving a court system that would assign guilt and recompense. However, the principles here go well beyond the court system; they're applicable to all of us who serve as judge, jury, and executioner of others in our hearts.

How do we file suit and then issue judgment of others in our hearts?

What kind of payment do we internally demand of others when we judge them?

When we judge others, even if it's just in our hearts, we also carry out the sentence. In our hearts we assign people to categories, demanding that they prove themselves over and over again to us before they've finally served their time and can be put back in good graces. This is a vivid example of what happens when we fail to remember the sinful way of life that Christ has brought us out of. The people on the other end of our judgment should receive our mercy, for this is the way Jesus has treated us. When we remember what we've been delivered from, we find ourselves less quick to climb the ladder of comparison, judging others based on what they've contributed to or taken from our personal lives.

Rather than issuing judgment, we're to intentionally lift up those we might previously have stood over in self-righteous pride. This is what James advocated in his letter.

Read James 4:1–12. According to James, how does pride affect our view of human dignity?

Among other things, the gospel puts all of us on equal footing. The ground is level at the foot of the cross, for all those who come to Christ can collectively and holistically be described as sinners. At the cross all worldly marks of success and prominence fade away, first in the abyss of our sinfulness and then in the matchless grace of God. James's congregation needed to be reminded of this, for all their fighting, quarreling, and warring had at their root the failure to remember who they were before God.

How do we know whether we have the kind of humility that will receive grace from the Lord? One of the most practical ways humility expresses itself is in the way we treat others the world would deem to be unworthy of respect and honor. It's no wonder, then, that the Book of James contains such practical instruction in regard to the way we treat these groups in society. Consider this verse:

> *Religion that is pure and undefiled before God, the Father, is this: to visit orphans and widows in their affliction, and to keep oneself unstained from the world.*
> **JAMES 1:27**

Does it surprise you to see James place so much emphasis on these two groups? Why or why not?

What does it mean to be stained by the world?
How does the command to be unstained fit with
the emphasis on caring for widows and orphans?

While it might surprise us at one level for James to highlight these two particular ministries, it underscores that our treatment of the overlooked and neglected is a true reflection of our view of ourselves before the Lord. For the church in the days of James, widows and orphans were throwaway people. Unable to support themselves or contribute to society, they were cultural leeches, hanging on only by the good graces of those gullible or sentimental enough to support them. The worldly approach to these two groups, then, would be to discard them. They would go the way of all useless things.

We typically think of worldliness in terms of moral impurity, and that's certainly a part of it, but in a larger sense, worldliness is thinking in the way of the world. In this particular instance the most antiworldly thing we can do is to welcome, value, and prioritize these people the rest of the world has no time or patience for. It's to do the opposite:

My brothers, show no partiality as you hold the faith in our Lord Jesus Christ, the Lord of glory. For if a man wearing a gold ring and fine clothing comes into your assembly, and a poor man in shabby clothing also comes in, and if you pay attention to the one who wears the fine clothing and say, "You sit here in a good place," while you say to the poor man, "You stand over there," or, "Sit down at my feet," have you not then made distinctions among yourselves and become judges with evil thoughts?
JAMES 2:1-4

What worldly attitude is displayed in these verses?

What would it look like to be unstained
by the world in this situation?

To be worldly in this instance is to show favoritism, prizing what the world deems as important. Instead, James reminded the church of the true worth and dignity afforded to all God's people.

Read James 2:5–13. What are some groups of people in our culture today we likely show favoritism to?

Why is this a gospel issue, not just a matter of favoritism?

There are other examples in church history of the church's standing in opposition to the patterns of the world. Take, for example, the time when the church was growing and flourishing in Jerusalem (see Acts 2:42-47) prior to the persecution that occurred after the death of Stephen. An issue arose among the widows of the community. Even within the fellowship of believers there was a class system, for the Greek widows were being neglected in favor of the Jewish widows (see Acts 6:1). When the issue was presented to the church leaders, it would have been very easy for them to disregard it as unimportant, given the class of people they were discussing. After all, they were very busy with the business of a growing congregation. But instead of ignoring the needs, they acknowledged them and took active measures to make sure kingdom priorities were lived out in their midst.

Read the church leaders' solution.

In these days when the disciples were increasing in number, a complaint by the Hellenists arose against the Hebrews because their widows were being neglected in the daily distribution. And the twelve summoned the full number of the disciples and said, "It is not right that we should give up preaching the word of God to serve tables. Therefore, brothers, pick out from among you seven men of good repute, full of the Spirit and of wisdom, whom we will appoint to this duty. But we will devote ourselves to prayer and to the ministry of the word."

ACTS 6:1-4

How did the apostles demonstrate the importance of this issue?

How does this solution help us see the holistic nature of the gospel?

It was not an either/or decision but rather a both/and. The solution described here provides for those being neglected, all the while making sure the gospel was continually preached. The gospel was declared and demonstrated, and the kingdom was modeled in their midst.

Addressing the issue of human dignity is a gospel issue. When we neglect it, we show we've forgotten that we all at one point were outside the realm of God's blessing. Once we were all poor. Once we were all enslaved. Once we were all spiritual orphans. But God, in the gospel, has made provision for us.

How should the gospel influence our response to a culture that doesn't share the same view of the dignity and value of human life?

Make a list of practical ways we can respond to injustice toward human life while declaring and demonstrating the gospel.

Issues of human dignity are much bigger than the way society normally views them. The basic need of all humankind is met only in the gospel of Jesus Christ.

KINGDOM CULTURE MISSION HUMAN DIGNITY FAMILY STABILITY CONVICTIONAL KINDNESS

START

Welcome to session 5 of *Onward*. Open your group time by asking participants to give quick answers to the following questions.

What was one thing that stood out to you as you worked through the personal study this week?

How has this focus on the issue of human dignity changed your perspective on people you've encountered this week?

In this session we'll focus on family stability. How have you seen the challenges to family stability change over the course of your lifetime?

We've seen that understanding the kingdom of God helps us shape the culture of the church and then rightly engage the culture of the world without compromising the gospel. Along with the issue of human dignity, we must also be a voice in the church and the world for the sake of family stability.

Read together as a group Psalm 127. Then watch video session 5, in which Dr. Moore teaches on family stability.

... *making known to us the* MYSTERY
of his will, according to his purpose,
which he set forth in CHRIST.
EPHESIANS 1:9

A man shall leave his father and mother and hold fast
to his wife, and the two shall become ONE FLESH.
EPHESIANS 5:31

You are no longer strangers and aliens,
but you are fellow citizens with the saints
and members of the HOUSEHOLD *of God.*
EPHESIANS 2:19

RESPOND

In the video Dr. Moore discussed how strange the Christian definition of *family* has become in modern culture. He also asked several questions that need to be answered in our lives and churches if our understanding of family is to keep in step with the gospel.

Why do we have families to begin with?

Why is answering this question pivotal for believers today? How will answering that question help us engage with the culture around us?

In what ways does the family relate to God's plan to create everything with Jesus at the center?

Dr. Moore shared an example from the Book of Ephesians that helped us see the higher and deeper purpose of marriage and family in general.

Read Ephesians 5:22–32. What deeper purpose of marriage is identified in these verses? In what ways does marriage reflect the gospel?

What are the implications of broken marriages? Why is the preponderance of broken marriages such a serious issue?

What are some ways we can make sure our churches are ready to receive people who find the cultural definition of family unfulfilling?

Pray, thanking God for His family in the church. Pray that the church, as the household of faith, will rightly demonstrate what it means to be part of the family of God.

Complete the three personal-study sections on the following pages before the next group session.

TEACHINGS OF JESUS

There's no such thing as the good old days. That reality is difficult for us to stomach because we tend to look at the past through rose-colored glasses. The bad times we experienced, from hindsight, weren't all that bad, and the good times were exponentially better when viewed in the rearview mirror. This is as true of our picture of the family as other areas of life.

In what ways do Christians tend to have a good–old–days mentality about the family?

Do you agree that this viewpoint is a myth? Why or why not?

Why is it important for us to recognize the myth if we want to actively engage the culture with a biblical view of the family?

We might look to significant points in history, such as the sexual revolution of the 1960s, the introduction of abortion, or the relative ease of obtaining a divorce, as pivotal moments when the family came under attack. The truth, though, is that the crisis in the family isn't downstream from Woodstock or the pill. Instead, it's downstream from the wreckage of the fall in Eden. The family is and has been under assault in every generation of human history though sometimes in less visible and more subtle ways. Take, for example, the question the Pharisees asked Jesus in Matthew 19.

Read the following passage and underline
the question the Pharisees asked Jesus.

*When Jesus had finished these sayings, he went away
from Galilee and entered the region of Judea beyond the
Jordan. And large crowds followed him, and he healed
them there. And Pharisees came up to him and tested
him by asking, "Is it lawful to divorce one's wife for
any cause?" He answered, "Have you not read that he
who created them from the beginning made them male
and female, and said, 'Therefore a man shall leave his
father and his mother and hold fast to his wife, and the
two shall become one flesh'? So they are no longer two
but one flesh. What therefore God has joined together,
let not man separate." They said to him, "Why then did
Moses command one to give a certificate of divorce and
to send her away?" He said to them, "Because of your
hardness of heart Moses allowed you to divorce your
wives, but from the beginning it was not so. And I
say to you: whoever divorces his wife, except for sexual
immorality, and marries another, commits adultery." The
disciples said to him, "If such is the case of a man with
his wife, it is better not to marry." But he said to them,
"Not everyone can receive this saying, but only those to
whom it is given. For there are eunuchs who have been
so from birth, and there are eunuchs who have been
made eunuchs by men, and there are eunuchs who have
made themselves eunuchs for the sake of the kingdom of
heaven. Let the one who is able to receive this receive it."*

MATTHEW 19:1-12

Did the Pharisees want a legitimate answer to this
question? What was their true motive in asking?

Why do you think Jesus responded the way He did?

In Jesus' day there was a tremendous amount of debate about divorce and remarriage among the Jews. Some rabbis said a man couldn't divorce his wife unless she'd been unfaithful. Others claimed a man could divorce his wife over much more trivial matters, from an improperly cooked meal to his selection of a more appealing mate. You could argue, then, that these Pharisees simply wanted a clarification from a touted religious leader of the time.

We know, however, that this was far from an innocent inquiry; it was a test (see v. 3). When the Pharisees tried to trap Jesus with a question about divorce, Jesus knew the issue was really about Him. As the Pharisees often did, they wanted to put Jesus in a difficult situation with the crowds, in which He'd seem to be exposed as outside God's revelation to Moses. This wasn't an honest question about views on marital permanence; it was a language-game trap.

Jesus wasn't interested in biting. Instead, he took His hearers back to the very beginning.

Why is it significant that the events in the Scriptures Jesus quoted (Gen. 1:27; 2:24) occurred prior to the giving of the Mosaic law?

What does this fact show us about God's intent for family?

Family was in God's design from the very beginning; He hardwired man and woman with a relational capacity that must be filled. The question from the Pharisees assumed the inevitability of divorce; Jesus was unwilling to make that allowance. In the beginning there was no such division in the family. The question in and of itself betrayed not only the sinfulness of the Pharisees asking it but also the fact that the family, along with everything else in creation, was broken at the fall.

The Pharisees weren't to be swayed:

*"Why then did Moses command one to give
a certificate of divorce and to send her away?"
He said to them, "Because of your hardness
of heart Moses allowed you to divorce your
wives, but from the beginning it was not so."*
MATTHEW 19:7-8

**Compare verses 7 and 8. Underline the word
command and the word *allowed*. What does the
difference between those two words show you?**

With the substitution of a single word, the Pharisees showed their error. Divorce, in the Old Testament, the New Testament, or anytime since, was never a command. The Scripture in question, Deuteronomy 24:1-4, was given as a concession because of the sinfulness of humanity. God didn't command or endorse divorce, but in His mercy He made an allowance for such an action. However, Jesus wanted to make sure, by taking us back prior to the law in the days when everything was just as it should be, that the current state of the family was never what God intended.

The Pharisees in this passage had made the mistake of adopting too low a view of the family, one in which a cultural norm had been accepted as permissible even among the people of God.

**What are some ways we make the same mistake
of taking too low a view of the family?**

**How has the church, like the Pharisees, made a
culturally permissible practice acceptable within
the body of Christ when it comes to family?**

In another account the Sadducees used a similar tactic with Jesus. This time, however, the view of family wasn't too low but too high.

Read that account in the following verses.

Sadducees came to him, who say that there is no resurrection. And they asked him a question, saying, "Teacher, Moses wrote for us that if a man's brother dies and leaves a wife, but leaves no child, the man must take the widow and raise up offspring for his brother. There were seven brothers; the first took a wife, and when he died left no offspring. And the second took her, and died, leaving no offspring. And the third likewise. And the seven left no offspring. Last of all the woman also died. In the resurrection, when they rise again, whose wife will she be? For the seven had her as wife."

MARK 12:18-23

Summarize the question the Sadducees asked Jesus.

How does their question reveal too high a view of the family?

The Sadducees made the mistake of elevating the family to the point of idolatry. In their minds the family had an existence outside the resurrection goal of a new creation. Jesus pointed out their false thinking and deception in His response:

Is this not the reason you are wrong, because you know neither the Scriptures nor the power of God? For when they rise from the dead, they neither marry nor are given in marriage, but are like angels in heaven. And as for the dead being raised, have you not read in the book of Moses, in the passage about the bush, how God spoke to him, saying, "I am the God of Abraham, and the God of Isaac, and the God of Jacob"? He is not God of the dead, but of the living. You are quite wrong.

MARK 12:24-27

The family isn't an end in itself. Issues of family stability are important, both inside the church and in the culture of the rest of the world. But we become derailed when we begin to treat temporal issues as eternal.

When we're armed with an understanding of the kingdom, however, we can rightly confront these issues not only for the sake of the family but also for the greater purposes of the kingdom. The Pharisees missed the alpha point of the Bible's story line: God's purposes in creation. The Sadduccees also missed the omega point of the Bible's story line: the meaning of the kingdom of God in the age to come. In both instances they were trying to interpret the family apart from God's purposes in Christ as the Alpha and Omega of creation. Unwilling to recognize Jesus as the Christ, they were unable to see where God's creational structures fit into the universe.

In other words, it's only through Jesus that we can rightly interpret the rest of the created order. That leads us back again to one of the core truths of the kingdom: God is creating everything around Jesus Christ as part of an inheritance for Him, including marriage, family, sexuality, gender, and everything else in creation.

What does it mean to you personally to interpret marriage, family, sexuality, gender, and everything else through Jesus? Why is this so important to understand?

How does this understanding change the way you approach views of the family that clash with your own?

What are areas in your life that you've failed to filter through the gospel? How has this neglect affected your life?

Apart from this foundational starting point, no matter what our outward commitment to a particular issue might appear to be, we'll be the kind of people Paul described in Romans 1:18-32 when he noted that those who refuse to give thanks as creatures ultimately turn to the creation itself with their worship. We mustn't do that. We must see family stability in light of the centrality of Jesus Christ. Otherwise, we become family idolaters in spite of our efforts to become family advocates.

WITNESS OF SCRIPTURE

The beginning point for understanding the issue of family stability is the kingdom of God. Instead of seeing family stability as an isolated issue worth defending in the culture, we must realign ourselves with the greater purposes of the kingdom in which family stability plays a significant role. This is what Paul did for the church at Ephesus.

It's true that throughout his letter to the Ephesians, Paul addressed specific dynamics of the relationships among husbands, wives, and children. He did so, however, by framing those specific issues in the larger context of God's kingdom so that his readers wouldn't become convinced that these earthly relationships are an end in and of themselves.

Paul's argument begins in chapter 1 with God's unveiling of the mystery of Christ:

In him we have redemption through his blood, the forgiveness of our trespasses, according to the riches of his grace, which he lavished upon us, in all wisdom and insight making known to us the mystery of his will, according to his purpose, which he set forth in Christ as a plan for the fullness of time, to unite all things in him, things in heaven and things on earth.
EPHESIANS 1:7-10

**In the previous verses underline what
God is bringing together in Christ.**

**What do you think is the significance of Paul's including
this teaching at the beginning of the letter, prior
to giving practical instruction about the family?**

By including this key teaching at the beginning of his letter, Paul set up everything that follows. No matter how detailed his other teachings might get, it all relates to this larger universal purpose of God. It might be helpful to think of the family, then, in terms of two arenas: the physical and the cosmic.

From the standpoint of the physical purposes, the family must function in harmony together for pragmatic reasons. A husband and a wife must have a sexual relationship in order to procreate and bear children. They must stay together in order to provide an environment of love and stability for their children. And they must love, submit to, and serve each other to make their home the best it can be.

These physical purposes of the family go only so far, though. In our thinking we must also elevate each of these purposes to the higher ground God intended. If God's overall purpose is to bring together all things in Christ, then the family must serve this higher, cosmic end. This is why, as Paul continued his letter into chapters 5–6, he didn't just give practical instruction for families but elevated our thinking into the cosmic realm.

Read the following verses.

As the church submits to Christ, so also wives should submit in everything to their husbands. Husbands, love your wives, as Christ loved the church and gave himself up for her, that he might sanctify her, having cleansed her by the washing of water with the word, so that he might present the church to himself in splendor, without spot or wrinkle or any such thing, that she might be holy and without blemish. In the same way husbands should love their wives as their own bodies. He who loves his wife loves himself. For no one ever hated his own flesh, but nourishes and cherishes it, just as Christ does the church, because we are members of his body. "Therefore a man shall leave his father and mother and hold fast to his wife, and the two shall become one flesh."
EPHESIANS 5:24-31

ONWARD

List the instructions Paul gave to wives and husbands.

Wives   Husbands

What does it mean to submit?

Should that word have a positive
or negative connotation? Why?

On a practical level Paul instructed wives to submit to their husbands (see v. 22). The word *submit* has fallen on hard times in our day; submission is equated with giving up one's personhood. A submissive wife is seen as a doormat who exists to meet the needs of her husband and family. But if you read Paul's instructions, you'll see that nothing could be further from the truth.

The submission Paul described is a willing submission, not one under compulsion. In fact, the submission is lovingly done in light of the instructions Paul gave to husbands. While the wife submits, the husband is called to love her (see v. 28). But he's not called to love in any old way; instead, his love is meant to emulate the love of Christ. To see the way a husband should function in marriage, then, we must look to Christ.

What are some ways we see the love of Christ?

How does Jesus' way of loving heighten the
love a husband should have toward his wife?

How does love like that affect submission in marriage?

How did Christ love? He loved unconditionally. He loved sacrificially. He loved even to death. In Christ we see a servant-hearted kind of love, love that prompted Him to give up His very life for the sake of the church (see v. 25). When love like that is actualized in marriage, submission moves from a compulsory duty to a joyous delight. In that kind of relationship, a wife can freely and lovingly submit to her husband's leadership because she's confident that he has her absolute best in mind. He wants to see her thrive, not give up her rights. We know this because it's the way Christ has treated us.

These are good instructions for how to have a harmonious marriage, but Paul isn't content to keep the discussion on a physical level. Rather, he elevates it, letting us know that the greater purpose of marriage isn't raising children. It's not companionship. It's not having a dual income for tax purposes. The greater purpose of marriage is to model the relationship of Jesus and His church. When people look at Christian marriage, they should see a walking, talking, living, breathing illustration of Jesus and the church. Ultimately, marriage is about the gospel.

When God instituted marriage in Genesis 2:21-25, the passage Paul quoted in these verses (see Eph. 5:31), He had the centrality of Jesus and the gospel in mind. He created a human relationship that would point to and highlight the greater marriage between Jesus and His people. Our earthly institutions model the heavenly reality. That pattern continues in Ephesians 6.

Read the following verses.

Children, obey your parents in the Lord, for this is right. "Honor your father and mother" (this is the first commandment with a promise), "that it may go well with you and that you may live long in the land." Fathers, do not provoke your children to anger, but bring them up in the discipline and instruction of the Lord.

EPHESIANS 6:1-4

What are the physical instructions Paul gave to children?
How about to fathers? List them in the columns below.

Children   Fathers

What spiritual reality does the
father–child relationship point to?

This passage gives practical instructions to both children and fathers, and the instructions are related to each other: children obey as fathers exercise discipline and guidance. Although the obedience of children isn't meant to be contingent on their fathers' patience, it certainly makes it a lot easier.

Like all things at their core, the issue is one of faith. Children come to the place where they obey their parents not only because it's good and right but also because they're confident in their parents' authority. They know their parents wouldn't abuse that authority but instead would lovingly instruct them in a way that's ultimately for their good, even if they don't understand how or why. Once again, though, Paul didn't leave us in the realm of the physical, although these practical instructions would certainly be helpful for developing healthy relationships between parents and their children. There's a higher purpose. Fathers are to "bring them up in the discipline and instruction of the Lord" (Eph. 6:4).

Think about the phrase "bring them up in
the discipline and instruction of the Lord."
What, in your own words, does that mean?

If you have children, what are some ways you attempt to do this?

In what ways can you follow this instruction more closely?

This phrase is about more than biblical principles, although that's certainly important. This phrase is about raising children in such a way that it's natural for them to call God their Father. Once again, our earthly constructs are meant to point to spiritual realities. The best example of God that children could have is their own father.

These are sobering thoughts for us in our families. It should take our breath away to think that our relationships are meant to model and point to heavenly realities and that both our marriages and our parenting point onlookers to the nature and characteristics of the kingdom. Let's not, then, take a merely pragmatic approach to family stability. Let's instead embrace the much weightier purpose God has in mind for us and understand that our families are meant to reflect relationships in His kingdom.

GOSPEL APPLICATION

As we've seen, Paul unfolded in the Book of Ephesians the greater purposes for the human family. Chapter 1 begins with the unveiling of the mystery of Christ, and as the letter continues, it demonstrates how this mystery explains our redemption (see chaps. 1–2), the makeup of the church (see chaps. 2–3), the ministry of the church (see chaps. 4–5), and our callings in our families (see chaps. 5–6). In Christ God achieved unity in one new Man for a humanity fractured by the fall (see 2:1-6). One key aspect of this unveiled mystery is that the family structure isn't an arbitrary expression of the will of God but an icon of God's purpose of the universe in Christ.

This area of family stability is one of the areas, at this particular moment in history, in which Christians are the most strange. To advance the kingdom without losing the gospel, the fight begins with us at a very personal level—that of sexuality.

How have you seen the discussion of sexuality change in your lifetime?

Mark a point on the scale to indicate your level of concern about issues of sexuality you see around you.

1	2	3	4	5
Not concerned at all			Very concerned	

Why is sexuality a spiritual issue? Why is it so important to have an accurate biblical understanding of sexuality?

One of our tendencies as humans is to divide areas of life into the secular and the sacred. For example, we might think of something like our daily prayers as spiritual but something like what we eat and how we exercise as secular. After all, God is concerned about the soul, right? Paul addressed this topic in 1 Corinthians 6:

"All things are lawful for me," but not all things are helpful. "All things are lawful for me," but I will not be dominated by anything. "Food is meant for the stomach and the stomach for food"—and God will destroy both one and the other. The body is not meant for sexual immorality, but for the Lord, and the Lord for the body. And God raised the Lord and will also raise us up by his power.
1 CORINTHIANS 6:12-14

Why did Paul use several quotations in this passage?

What are some key principles Paul introduced in this passage?

God didn't intend a division between the sacred and secular. Just as Christ is saving our souls, He's also redeeming our bodies. The kingdom of God isn't just a spiritual reality but a physical one, and that means issues about our personal sexuality and the way we treat our bodies have profound spiritual implications. In these verses Paul began with the common subject of food, reminding us that just because it might be permissible to eat in any number of ways, it's not necessarily advisable. To make his point, Paul employed some common phrases in the Corinthian culture that essentially gave permission to people to pursue what they desired.

In the kingdom, however, there's a much different ethic. To decide what, when, and how much to eat, we should do more than glance at our body-mass index or a calorie counter. We should instead recognize the spiritual implications of our bodies.

Does that mean a decision whether to eat a chocolate bar is actually a spiritual decision? Yes, it does. When we have a holistic view of the kingdom, we come to realize that we can't make what seem to be momentary physical decisions without the kingdom of God and who we are in it in the background. If this is true about chocolate, then how much more must it be true with something as serious as our sexuality?

Keep reading Paul's words in 1 Corinthians 6:15–20.

Do you not know that your bodies are members of Christ? Shall I then take the members of Christ and make them members of a prostitute? Never! Or do you not know that he who is joined to a prostitute becomes one body with her? For, as it is written, "The two will become one flesh." But he who is joined to the Lord becomes one spirit with him. Flee from sexual immorality. Every other sin a person commits is outside the body, but the sexually immoral person sins against his own body. Or do you not know that your body is a temple of the Holy Spirit within you, whom you have from God? You are not your own, for you were bought with a price. So glorify God in your body.
1 CORINTHIANS 6:15-20

What does it mean and what's the significance when Paul says, "You are not your own, for you were bought with a price. So glorify God in your body" (vv. 19–20)?

Practically, how can we "flee from sexual immorality" (v. 18)?

To grasp the full implications of what Paul was saying, we need to remember two key truths.

1. OUR BODIES ARE A PART OF CHRIST'S BODY. Through the gospel we've been united with Christ, and His Spirit dwells in us. Therefore, we're truly the body of Christ as the church. Our physical bodies aren't our own; they've been claimed and purchased with the blood of Jesus.

When we choose the road of sexual immorality, it's more than inadvisable; we're taking a part of Christ's body and uniting it in an unholy way. Make no mistake: sexual action is indeed a union; that's why sex is an act reserved for marriage— the lifelong union between one man and one woman. When two people have a sexual encounter, it's a deeply spiritual moment, one in which two people become united with each other forever. This is why such an act is sacredly reserved for the covenant relationship of marriage. Anything else is a betrayal not only of the human institution of marriage but also of the spiritual reality of the body of Christ.

> ### How does sexual immorality show a disregard not only for Christ's body but also for other people?

2. WHEN WE CAME TO CHRIST, GOD FILLED US WITH HIS HOLY SPIRIT. In the Old Testament the Israelites built a temple that was to be the dwelling place of God. The temple was constructed as a series of concentric structures, each with more limited access than the previous one, until only one person could move into the most holy place and then only once a year.

The New Testament also sets up a temple. The new temple is the body of a Christian. The Holy Spirit of God has made His home in us. In the Book of Ephesians, Paul prayed that his readers would recognize this reality:

> *I bow my knees before the Father, from whom every family in heaven and on earth is named, that according to the riches of his glory he may grant you to be strengthened with power through his Spirit in your inner being, so that Christ may dwell in your hearts through faith.*
> **EPHESIANS 3:14-17**

Verse 17 is a prayer that Christ would be at home in our hearts. We should live in a way that recognizes the dwelling of Christ in us so that He can truly be at home in us, the new temple. The conclusion for us is that sexual expression isn't simply a matter of neurons firing. A Christian view of reality means that the body is a temple, set apart to be a dwelling place for the Holy Spirit. Sexual immorality, then, isn't just bad for us (although it is); it's also an act that desecrates a holy place.

Make a list of sexual sins you see as growing concerns in our culture today.

How can you protect your temple from the sexual sins you listed?

Our job as the church of Jesus is to help one another remember these things in a day and time when society's sexual ethic is constantly changing.

What are some ways we can help one another remember biblical truths about our sexuality?

Why do you think it's often so difficult or even awkward to help one another guard our temples from sexual sin?

In the church we don't just model this message. We live it. This is because the church itself, even apart from the individual family units represented in it, is actually a family:

> *You are no longer strangers and aliens, but you*
> *are fellow citizens with the saints and members*
> *of the household of God, built on the foundation*
> *of the apostles and prophets, Christ Jesus himself*
> *being the cornerstone, in whom the whole structure,*
> *being joined together, grows into a holy temple in*
> *the Lord. In him you also are being built together*
> *into a dwelling place for God by the Spirit.*
> **EPHESIANS 2:19-22**

Because we're God's household, His family, the message of family stability isn't just for wives, husbands, fathers, and mothers. It's also for those in God's family who might remain single or never bear children of their own.

A woman might never marry or have children, but she nonetheless mothers the body of Christ. A man might never father children physically and yet be a spiritual father for many in the church. Holistically, the way we treat one another in the church reflects this family dynamic. In a culture that prizes independence and privacy, these kinds of familial relationships that cross over bloodlines are indeed strange. But that's the point.

If we're strangers in this world, our family stability should reflect that same reality.

KINGDOM CULTURE

MISSION

HUMAN DIGNITY

FAMILY STABILITY

CONVICTIONAL KINDNESS

START

Welcome to session 6 of *Onward*. Open your group time by asking participants to give quick answers to the following questions.

What was one thing that stood out to you as you worked through the personal study this week?

If someone asked you why issues of family are important for Christians, how would you respond in light of what you studied this week?

In this session we'll focus on the nature of our engagement with the culture—convictional kindness. What do you think is the difference between being nice and being kind?

As we move into the culture and engage with others on important issues like the ones we've discussed, it's important that we focus not only on the content of our arguments but also on the tone with which we express ourselves. For Christians, that tone is one of convictional kindness in our interactions.

Read together as a group John 3:16-21. Then watch video session 6, in which Dr. Moore teaches on convictional kindness.

WATCH

*The Lord's servant must not be quarrelsome
but* KIND *to* EVERYONE.
2 TIMOTHY 2:24

*God did not send his Son into the world
to* CONDEMN THE WORLD, *but in order
that the world* MIGHT BE SAVED *through him.*
JOHN 3:17

Behold, the LAMB OF GOD, *who
takes away the* SIN OF THE WORLD!
JOHN 1:29

What have I to do with JUDGING
OUTSIDERS? *Is it not those* INSIDE
THE CHURCH *whom you are to judge?*
1 CORINTHIANS 5:12

RESPOND

In the video Dr. Moore stated that interactions of calmness and kindness are unusual in today's culture, especially when it comes to the kinds of issues we've discussed.

Why do you think we tend to be argumentative when talking about these issues?

What are some challenges to discussing issues like these with convictional kindness?

Why can't we measure our level of conviction by our level of outrage?

Dr. Moore pointed us to Jesus, who showed us the right and wrong times to be outraged. In the Gospels we're often surprised because the times we expect to see Jesus outraged, He's calm, and the times we expect to see Him calm, He's outraged.

Read Matthew 21:12–13. Why was Jesus outraged?

Conversely, why was Jesus calm when dealing with people found in sin, like the woman at the well in John 4?

How does a firm understanding of and confidence in the kingdom of God allow us to engage other people with kindness?

Which of the issues we've talked about over the course of this study is the most difficult for you to talk about with kindness? Why?

Pray, thanking God that we can engage with people about these issues from a position of confidence, knowing the gates of hell won't overcome the church of Jesus Christ.

Complete the three personal-study sections on the following pages to conclude your study of *Onward*.

TEACHINGS OF JESUS

If you're a parent, you're likely familiar with matters of tone. One of the things children have to learn is that tone can actually be more important than the actual content of the message itself. That's why teenagers might get into an equal amount of trouble when they give the right answer in a disrespectful tone as they would have if the actual content been offensive. Our posture matters; in fact, our posture might reveal even more than the message we give verbally.

As Christians, therefore, we must consider not only the content of what we say to the culture around us but also the tone with which we express ourselves. Paul reminds us:

> *In Christ God was reconciling the world to himself, not counting their trespasses against them, and entrusting to us the message of reconciliation. Therefore, we are ambassadors for Christ, God making his appeal through us. We implore you on behalf of Christ, be reconciled to God.*
> **2 CORINTHIANS 5:19-20**

What kind of tone was Paul advocating in these verses?

Think about your usual tone when you engage
the culture about some of the issues we've
studied. Mark where you'd fall on the scale.

1	2	3	4	5
Violently angry				Accepting without confrontation

What are some of the motivating factors behind your rating?

Of course, when we look to Jesus, we find the right and proper way to engage the culture. Jesus modeled the uncompromising truth and unwavering kindness we need as He encountered the culture. This tone, expressed countless times not only through His words but also through His actions, was disturbing to His opponents. They couldn't understand how He'd interact so kindly with people many thought were better cast out of their society. One of the best examples we have is His encounter with a Samaritan woman.

Read John 4:1–26. How would you describe the woman's tone in this account?

How would you describe Jesus' tone toward her?

The first significant detail in this account lies simply in the fact that Jesus approached this woman at all. For His people, the pure-blooded Jews, such an interaction with a Samaritan, much less a woman, was unthinkable. Speaking to a Samaritan woman, whom many would have seen as a dog, was a lowering of God-given status, and the woman knew it. This is the reason for her incredulous response to Jesus' request for some water.

This woman knew about Jews; she knew they looked down their noses at people like her, all because of her bloodline. Yet Jesus was willing to cross over centuries of animosity built up by pride and the corresponding resentment to actually have a simple conversation with this woman.

Identify any groups of people in your life
that you might be hostile toward, either because
of pride on your part or pride on their part.

How does such an attitude run
against the truth of the gospel?

The gospel was precisely the subject of the conversation, although the woman
didn't know it at first. While she was still surprised by the interaction, Jesus elevated her thinking from the physical subject of water to a far more spiritual one.
He verbally lanced her at her point of greatest insecurity, and yet He did it all with
kindness. With a gracious tone He was able not only to speak to her about who He
was but also to confront her sin in an unflinching manner.

There's an important lesson here for us: kindness doesn't mean an avoidance of
difficult issues. Surely for this woman, there was no more difficult or sensitive issue
in her life than her past sexual history. Jesus didn't shy away from that subject
because it was impolite to discuss such issues; He told her the truth, but He told it
to her in a kind manner, framing His words with the good news of who He was and is.

We can easily become confused, thinking if we're being kind, we should avoid
issues of great importance in our dialogue with those outside the Christian faith.
Nothing could be further from the truth. We see in Jesus a willingness to engage
in the most sensitive and even potentially awkward subjects; we see from those
He engaged with a willingness not only to hear but also to believe. How was Jesus
able to do this? The answer is tone.

What evidence do you see in this passage that Jesus'
tone was effective in communicating His message?

Think about the opposite perspective. How might Jesus have approached this encounter with a less gracious tone?

This wasn't the only time Jesus exemplified convictional kindness toward those considered to be sinners and outsiders. Consider the encounter He had with the tree-climbing tax collector named Zacchaeus.

Read the account of Jesus and Zacchaeus in the following passage.

He entered Jericho and was passing through. And behold, there was a man named Zacchaeus. He was a chief tax collector and was rich. And he was seeking to see who Jesus was, but on account of the crowd he could not, because he was small in stature. So he ran on ahead and climbed up into a sycamore tree to see him, for he was about to pass that way. And when Jesus came to the place, he looked up and said to him, "Zacchaeus, hurry and come down, for I must stay at your house today." So he hurried and came down and received him joyfully. And when they saw it, they all grumbled, "He has gone in to be the guest of a man who is a sinner." And Zacchaeus stood and said to the Lord, "Behold, Lord, the half of my goods I give to the poor. And if I have defrauded anyone of anything, I restore it fourfold." And Jesus said to him, "Today salvation has come to this house, since he also is a son of Abraham. For the Son of Man came to seek and to save the lost."

LUKE 19:1-10

What similarities do you notice between Jesus' interactions with Zacchaeus and the Samaritan woman?

Just as the Samaritans were considered beneath the level of Jesus' ethnic people, tax collectors were considered to be on the bottom rung of people Jesus might have chosen to associate with. Tax collectors like Zacchaeus were traitors to their own people, having chosen to align themselves with the occupying Romans for financial gain. In addition, tax collectors were notoriously dishonest, skimming money off the top of the taxes they'd collected. For reasons like these, you'd be hard-pressed to find a more hated group of people at that time.

We should notice in this account just how thick the crowd was. Evidently, so many people were seeking to get a glimpse of Jesus that the diminutive Zacchaeus had to shimmy up a tree to see this new kind of rabbi. I'm sure everyone was shocked to hear the words that came out of Jesus' mouth next:

Zacchaeus, hurry and come down,
for I must stay at your house today.
LUKE 19:5

How did the other people respond to Jesus' words? What does their reaction reveal about their hearts?

Look closely at Jesus' statement in verse 5. Was this a request? Why is Jesus' language significant?

This wasn't a request for lodging; it was a divine imperative. Jesus' *had* to stay at Zacchaeus's house, and the reason comes in verse 10:

The Son of Man came to seek and to save the lost.
LUKE 19:10

**How do Jesus' actions challenge you in the way
you show kindness and grace to others?**

**What are potential ways you'll need to suffer
and sacrifice in the future so that others will
be able to hear the good news of Jesus?**

**What agendas currently dominate your heart that need
to die in order to make room for convictional kindness?**

The divine imperative of Jesus' association with Zacchaeus was driven by Jesus' mission. If He came "to seek and to save the lost," then of course Jesus must stay with Zacchaeus, even if it meant moving past all the other potential people He might have stayed with who were jam-packed on the side of the Jericho road. While others were grumbling, Zacchaeus couldn't believe the generosity and kindness shown to him; he welcomed Jesus joyfully (see v. 6).

Does this mean we can expect the same kind of joyous welcome that Jesus received? Of course not, for Jesus Himself was not always welcomed with that response. However, it does mean if we've adopted the mission of the kingdom, the tone we take with the culture around us should have the same ring of convictional kindness that dominated the interactions of the King we follow.

WITNESS OF SCRIPTURE

We've seen in the life of Jesus a remarkable ability to be kind to those He encountered even while boldly speaking the truth. Too often we fail to follow Jesus in this aspect of His mission. Instead of taking the posture of an ambassador, pleading with all to be reconciled to God (see 2 Cor. 5:20), we take an adversarial posture. We equate our measure of conviction with our level of outrage; the more conviction we have, the louder and angrier we think we can present our argument.

Our challenge, then, is to cultivate the kind of convictional kindness in our witness that we see in Jesus. This kindness isn't weak or passive. In fact, kindness is an act of spiritual warfare. Nowhere is this fact better revealed than in the instruction of Paul to his son in the faith, the young pastor Timothy.

Read the following verses. Below each one briefly record Paul's instruction to Timothy.

1 Timothy 1:18

1 Timothy 4:14

1 Timothy 6:12

2 Timothy 1:8

2 Timothy 2:3

What do all these instructions have in common?

The apostle Paul, drawing near to the end of his life and ministry, wrote letters to Timothy and Titus, who'd carry on the mission. Timothy, leading the church in Ephesus, from the context of the letters sent to him, was plagued with a personal vulnerability to timidity and fear. Paul, imprisoned and heading for execution, continually urged his protégé to "wage the good warfare" (1 Tim. 1:18), "not neglect the gift you have" (1 Tim. 4:14), "fight the good fight of the faith" (1 Tim. 6:12), "not be ashamed" (2 Tim. 1:8), and be "a good soldier of Christ Jesus" (2 Tim. 2:3). The old apostle had to counsel Timothy through his stomach problems (see 1 Tim. 5:23) right after instructing him in how to rebuke persistent sin in the ranks (see 1 Tim. 5:20). He had to tell him to let no one despise his youth (see 1 Tim. 4:12), reminding him:

God gave us a spirit not of fear but of power and love and self-control.
2 TIMOTHY 1:7

Paul's persistent message to Timothy was to have courage to fight, fight, fight. And then the apostle talked about kindness. He wasn't changing the subject. Kindness was the weapon he meant for Timothy to wield in spiritual warfare:

The Lord's servant must not be quarrelsome but kind to everyone, able to teach, patiently enduring evil, correcting his opponents with gentleness. God may perhaps grant them repentance leading to a knowledge of the truth, and they may come to their senses and escape from the snare of the devil, after being captured by him to do his will.
2 TIMOTHY 2:24-26

In the previous passage underline the characteristics God's servant is meant to embody.

Now read 1 Peter 2:17.

Honor everyone. Love the brotherhood. Fear God. Honor the emperor.
1 PETER 2:17

What similarities do you see between
1 Peter 2:17 and 2 Timothy 2:24–26?

Why is kindness an expression of spiritual warfare?

We typically don't think of kindness as a weapon; instead, we think of kindness as the exact opposite. But remember: we're citizens of and ambassadors for a different kind of kingdom from the world. It would only make sense, then, that the weapons at our disposal aren't the weapons of destruction the world uses.

In the same way Jesus Himself wasn't the political revolutionary the people of His day expected but instead a Suffering Servant, we must be committed to engage in the culture war in a different way than the rest of the world fights. Also remember:

> *We do not wrestle against flesh and blood, but*
> *against the rulers, against the authorities, against*
> *the cosmic powers over this present darkness, against*
> *the spiritual forces of evil in the heavenly places.*
> **EPHESIANS 6:12**

In our fight against these principalities, we fight with the fruit the Holy Spirit yields in our lives:

> *The fruit of the Spirit is love, joy, peace, patience,*
> *kindness, goodness, faithfulness, gentleness, self-*
> *control; against such things there is no law.*
> **GALATIANS 5:22-23**

We actually wage war with the fruit—love, joy, peace, patience, kindness, gentleness, and self-control—the Holy Spirit has cultivated in our lives.

To understand how to wage warfare with the fruit of the Spirit, we must understand two key principles about the nature of this war in which we're engaged.

1. REALIZE WHAT TRUE VICTORY LOOKS LIKE. Victory for God's kingdom isn't the Christianizing of society; it's not the return of the moral majority. Victory looks like people from every tribe, tongue, nation, and people worshiping at the throne of the Lamb. In the Book of Revelation, the apostle John described a scene in the throne room of heaven in which the four living creatures and the 24 elders worshiped the Lamb of God:

> *Worthy are you to take the scroll*
> *   and to open its seals,*
> *for you were slain, and by your blood*
> *you ransomed people for God*
> *   from every tribe and language*
> *and people and nation,*
> *and you have made them a kingdom*
> *and priests to our God,*
> *   and they shall reign on the earth.*
> **REVELATION 5:9-10**

It's very easy to get sidetracked as to what our true, broader mission is and to begin equating victory with the exercise of power. This power is precisely what the church is to be against. We don't persuade our neighbors by creating our own sanitized version of angry power protests; we don't win arguments by bringing corporations to the ground in surrender. That's the way of the world. In God's kingdom we offer a word of faithful witness that doesn't blink before the powers of the world but doesn't seek to imitate it either. In a day that's bent on achieving and then abusing this kind of power, the church is strange indeed when we practice convictional kindness even toward those who violently disagree with our positions on key issues for the culture.

Why is it so easy to confuse what our true mission is?

What would the church look like if we were
more concerned with a worldly kind of victory
than the spiritual victory of the kingdom?

What are some ways you can remind yourself of
what true victory looks like for God's kingdom?

Jesus Christ didn't "cry aloud or lift up his voice" (Isa. 42:2), and neither did He …

> *grow faint or [become] discouraged,*
> *till he [had] established justice in the earth.*
> **ISAIAH 42:4**

Jesus didn't defend Himself against personal offenses, and He didn't allow injustice to stand without shining light on it. He had a broader vision of what was going on. Jesus didn't blink before Pilate, because He knew He was ultimately setting the agenda, not Pilate (see John 18:36-37). He recognized the fight before him, but He also saw a bigger, more protracted fight in the distance. Kindness and gentleness grow, not when we downplay warfare but when we emphasize it. For Paul, kindness wasn't politeness. It was a weapon of spiritual warfare. We teach and rebuke with kindness and gentleness so that:

> *God may perhaps grant them repentance leading*
> *to a knowledge of the truth, and they may come*
> *to their senses and escape from the snare of the*
> *devil, after being captured by him to do his will.*
> **2 TIMOTHY 2:25-26**

2. THE PEOPLE WITH WHOM WE ENGAGE AREN'T OUR TRUE OPPONENTS.
In fact, they might just be our allies in waiting.

Look back at 2 Timothy 2:24–26. How did Paul
describe opponents of the truth in these verses?

Why do you think Paul was able to look with such hope and kindness on those to whom he was referring?

Sometimes we forget that the man who wrote these words was a reformed terrorist. The greatest apologist and missionary for the sake of Christ in human history spent a large part of his life trying to stamp out the very movement he later gave his life to advance. It's no wonder, then, that Paul could look at these opponents of the truth and remember himself.

Paul was the one who held the cloaks of those who murdered Stephen (see Acts 22:20). He was the one who was feared by the church because of his murderous intents (see 9:26). He was the one who was so blinded by his pride and rage that he was willing to take the lives of men, women, and children (see 9:1-2). Yet he was the one who came face-to-face with Truth Incarnate. It wasn't a far stretch for him, then, to see those around him as future believers.

How did Paul's past change the way he interacted with those outside the faith?

Think about your own journey to Jesus. How does your experience either positively or negatively affect the way you deal with people outside the faith?

Of course, not all of us have a dramatic conversion story like Paul. But we'd do well to remind ourselves that we ourselves were once citizens of a different kingdom. Our eyes have been opened to the truth, but that's not because of our personal résumé; it's because of the grace of God in Christ. That's also the case with everyone we interact with. These people aren't our opponents; they're potentially our future allies by God's grace. We should treat them with the kind of convictional kindness that reflects our belief that there are no lost causes when it comes to the mercy of God.

GOSPEL APPLICATION

Believers in Jesus aren't meant to be walking bumper stickers in our public witness, especially in regard to issues of righteousness and justice. We think this way sometimes. After all, these issues are of great importance, and in our age nothing signals conviction and passion more than the art of being theatrically offended.

This isn't the way of Jesus. He's the fulfillment of the word of the prophet Isaiah, quoted by the Gospel writer Matthew:

> *Behold, my servant whom I have chosen,*
>   *my beloved with whom my soul is well pleased.*
> *I will put my Spirit upon him,*
>   *and he will proclaim justice to the Gentiles.*
> *He will not quarrel or cry aloud,*
>   *nor will anyone hear his voice in the streets;*
> *a bruised reed he will not break,*
>   *and a smoldering wick he will not quench,*
> *until he brings justice to victory;*
>   *and in his name the Gentiles will hope.*
> **MATTHEW 12:18-21**

What was most striking about Jesus' tone as expressed in this prophecy?

What aspects of Jesus' character were reflected in His demeanor?

No one could argue with the passion and conviction of Jesus; those qualities aren't in question. His passion and conviction drove Him all the way to the cross. And yet He expressed that passion and conviction in a radically different way than we're accustomed to. It seems the loudest voice doesn't always win.

If the vehemence of our outrage were a clear sign of godliness, then the Devil would be the godliest soul in the cosmos.

Read the following verse and underline words that express the Devil's tone.

Woe to you, O earth and sea, for the devil has come down to you in great wrath, because he knows that his time is short!
REVELATION 12:12

What's the reason for the Devil's outrage in these verses?

How does that contrast with the reason for Jesus' calm patience?

The Devil rages and roars "because he knows that his time is short" (Rev. 12:12). Contrast him with the Lord Jesus, who didn't "quarrel or cry aloud" (Matt. 12:19). Why such a difference? Because the Devil has no mission apart from killing, destroying, accusing, and slandering. And because the Devil is on the losing side of history. Because he knows his time is short, he operates at a feverish, frenetic pace. Jesus, on the other hand, is willing to patiently play the long game, for He knows that ultimately it's indeed finished, and He's the victor along with His brothers and sisters.

As the church, we have the incredible luxury of operating from a position of victory. That knowledge changes everything about the way we engage with the culture around us.

Read the following account from Jesus' ministry on earth.

When Jesus came into the district of Caesarea Philippi, he asked his disciples, "Who do people say that the Son of Man is?" And they said, "Some say John the Baptist, others say Elijah, and others Jeremiah or one of the prophets." He said to them, "But who do you say that I am?" Simon Peter replied, "You are the Christ, the Son of the living God."
MATTHEW 16:13-16

**Why is it significant that Jesus required a personal
answer from His disciples to His question in verse 15?**

**Why is this question a pivotal one
for the entire world to answer?**

Jesus began this discourse with His disciples in the realm of generalities.
He wondered aloud who the crowds following Him thought He was. What were
the rumors? What was the general feeling? The answers abounded, just as they
do today:

- ★ He's a great teacher.
- ★ He's a prophet.
- ★ He's a misguided revolutionary.

**What other answers might you get if
you asked people today who Jesus is?**

Jesus wasn't content to talk about popular opinion. He instead turned His gaze on
the personal confession of the disciples, asking them the single most important
question anyone in the world will ever have to answer: "Who do you say that I
am?" (v. 15). Peter gave the right response, although he didn't fully understand
the implications of what he was saying. Jesus, however, built on Peter's confession
and gave all His future followers the confidence needed to engage with people
who might have a different opinion as to who He is:

> *Blessed are you, Simon Bar-Jonah! For flesh and
> blood has not revealed this to you, but my Father
> who is in heaven. And I tell you, you are Peter, and
> on this rock I will build my church, and the gates
> of hell shall not prevail against it. I will give you
> the keys of the kingdom of heaven, and whatever
> you bind on earth shall be bound in heaven, and
> whatever you loose on earth shall be loosed in heaven.*
> **MATTHEW 16:17-19**

Feel the weight of this statement for a moment. Try as they might, and they'll indeed try, the forces of darkness and the Devil will never overcome the church of Jesus Christ. This is why, no matter what the circumstances, every Christian can remain confident. This confidence isn't a starry-eyed optimism that's out of touch with reality; instead, it's a recognition that true victory can't be measured in terms of physical life and death but will extend for all eternity. In fact, circumstantial troubles and threats that face the church only serve to highlight the eternal nature of our message and our Lord's kingdom.

Read the following passage.

We have this treasure in jars of clay, to show that the surpassing power belongs to God and not to us. We are afflicted in every way, but not crushed; perplexed, but not driven to despair; persecuted, but not forsaken; struck down, but not destroyed; always carrying in the body the death of Jesus, so that the life of Jesus may also be manifested in our bodies. For we who live are always being given over to death for Jesus' sake, so that the life of Jesus also may be manifested in our mortal flesh. So death is at work in us, but life in you.
2 CORINTHIANS 4:7-12

Which part of these verses do you most resonate with? Why?

Why is God's plan for Christians to carry around the message of life in broken, fragile jars?

In our culture today we'll also feel pressured, perplexed, persecuted, and struck down. But despite those circumstances we'll never ultimately be crushed, despairing, abandoned, or destroyed. The church will prevail. One of the most dramatic effects of this firm belief is borne out in the tone we take with the culture around us.

When does someone cry and yell? When do they rage and flail? When they find themselves in a position of desperation, afraid and unsure of their future. If we find ourselves in an incontrollable rage, we'd do well to ask whether our anger truly comes from God or from man.

Read James 1:19–20.

Let every person be quick to hear, slow to speak, slow to anger; for the anger of man does not produce the righteousness of God.
JAMES 1:19-20

What are some traits of human anger? What's it rooted in?

What's the difference between that kind of anger and the righteous anger Jesus sometimes expressed in the Gospels?

As we examine ourselves, we might just find that the source of our anger isn't the righteous Jesus we claim to follow but instead a matter of our own insecurity or pride. We might be operating from a position of fear, fretting over the state or direction of our nation or our loss of respect or status. Or we might be so committed to our own viewpoint that what started out as righteous conviction has drifted into a personal vendetta. This isn't what God intends for His kingdom.

We aren't those people. We're people who are confident in the King and the kingdom He's created. Because we are, we can wage warfare from a position of victory, and the weapons at our disposal come in the form of convictional kindness to those around us.

As we express this kindness, however, we must remember that it won't lead to a lessening of controversy but a heightening of it. Although we might practice kindness, calling people to repentance, we'll be seen as mean or evil when we engage with the culture and stand for biblical truth. Jesus told us to expect this result:

A disciple is not above his teacher, nor a servant above his master. It is enough for the disciple to be like his teacher, and the servant like his master. If they have called the master of the house Beelzebul, how much more will they malign those of his household.
MATTHEW 10:24-25

The issue is whether we're *actually* mean or evil. That's what we can control. Of course, the best way we can control this is by making sure as we address issues in our culture, we don't stop there. Instead, we constantly beat the drum of the gospel. This is the true message of the kingdom.

Are there belief systems in culture you oppose and approach with a mean spirit? What are they? Reflect on some of the teachings in this study as you explain why this attitude doesn't reflect the gospel message.

List a couple of ways this study has made you reconsider the way you engage with the culture around you.

The gospel commands us to speak, and that speech is often forceful. But a prophetic witness in the new-covenant era never stops with "You brood of vipers!" (Matt. 3:7). It always continues to say:

Behold, the Lamb of God, who takes away the sin of the world!
JOHN 1:29

We make arguments, even as we understand that arguments are merely the equivalent of brush clearing to get to the main point: a personal connection with the voice that rings down through the ages from Nazareth. We want not simply to convey truth claims but to do so with the northern-Galilean accent that makes demons scream and chains fall. Kindness isn't surrender. Gentleness isn't passivity. Kindness and gentleness, rooted in gospel conviction—that's war.

NOTES

....
....
....
....
....
....
....
....
....
....
....
....
....
....
....
....
....
....
....
....
....
....
....
....

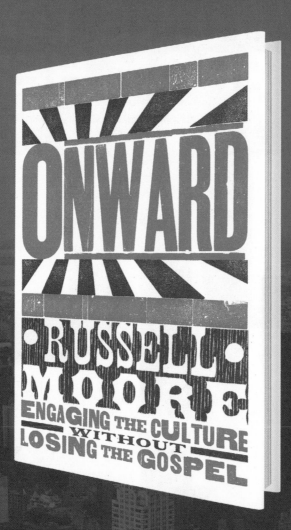

As the culture changes all around us, it is no longer possible to pretend that we are a Moral Majority. That may be bad news for America, but it can be good news for the church. What's needed now, in shifting times, is neither a doubling-down on the status quo nor a pullback into isolation. Instead, we need a church that speaks to social and political issues with a bigger vision in mind: that of the gospel of Jesus Christ. As Christianity seems increasingly strange, and even subversive, to our culture, we have the opportunity to reclaim the freakishness of the gospel, which is what gives it it's power in the first place.

VISIT RUSSELLMOORE.COM/ONWARD TO LEARN MORE

Every WORD Matters®
BHPublishingGroup.com

WHERE TO GO FROM HERE

Now that you've completed this study, here are a few possible directions you can go for your next one.

PARENTING

PRAYER

FIGHTING FEAR

Plumb the Bible's wisdom about parenting, discipline, the role of the church, and shaping a child's heart toward the gospel. (7 sessions)

Achieve a better understanding and approach to prayer through the prayers of Paul. (8 sessions)

Learn to dismantle the fears that steer you away from your God-given dreams. (6 sessions)